PRACTICAL HANDBOOK

THE COOK'S GUIDE TO
VEGETABLES

CHRISTINE INGRAM

HERMES
HOUSE

This edition published by Hermes House
an imprint of Anness Publishing Limited
Hermes House, 88-89 Blackfriars Road,
London SE1 8HA

ISBN 1 84038 842 0

A CIP catalogue record for this book is available from the
British Library

Publisher: Joanna Lorenz
Senior Cookery Editor: Linda Fraser
Editor: Rosemary Wilkinson
Designer: Patrick McLeavey
Food for Photography: Jane Stevenson
Photography and Styling: Patrick McLeavey and Thomas Odulate
Production Controller: Don Campaniello

Previously published as, *The Vegetable Ingredients Cookbook*

Printed and bound in Hong Kong

© Anness Publishing Limited 1996, 1999
Updated © 2000
1 3 5 7 9 10 8 6 4 2

NOTES

For all recipes, quantities are given in both metric and imperial
measures and, where appropriate, measures are also given in standard
cups and spoons. Follow one set, but not a mixture because they are
not interchangeable.

Standard spoon and cup measures are level.
1 tsp = 5ml, 1 tbsp = 15ml, 1 cup = 250ml/8fl oz

Medium eggs should be used unless otherwise stated.

Contents

INTRODUCTION

As a child, there were two basic types of vegetables for me: the ones my mother cooked and the ones given to us at school. My mother only ever bought fresh vegetables and she knew how to cook them, so they were simple but good. Vegetables at school were invariably horrible for equal but opposite reasons. Travel then broadened my outlook.

From my first teenage sojourns around Europe, I recall, even now, the stalls in a Barcelona produce market, piled high with tomatoes, peppers and aubergines. The exotic-looking produce of The Orient, Asia and Caribbean countries cannot fail to spark off an inquisitive, creative enthusiasm in those who are unfamiliar with them and even basic ingredients - potatoes, onions and carrots - do not look like sorry, everyday necessities when they are displayed with pride.

HISTORY

Plants have formed an essential part of our diet since the early existence of mankind. Hunter-gatherers progressed towards a more settled life as they learned how to cultivate crops and rear animals. Archaeological evidence indicates that forms of wheat and barley, believed to be the first crops, were farmed in the Middle East as early as 8000 BC. Many edible plants are native to this area, so we can assume that vegetables were also eaten, not least to relieve a monotonous diet.

As plants became a regular part of the diet for satisfying appetites, and those that caused stomach upsets were discovered and avoided, people realized the necessity of growing edible crops. Beans and

Left: Italian Roast Peppers.
Above: Roast Asparagus Crêpes.

Left: Shallots.

were commonly grown.

By the Middle Ages, a wealth of vegetables was available and recipes for them were recorded in the first cookery books.

Early explorers displayed exotic ingredients, the spoils of their travels, in their native countries and created a huge appetite for new tastes among the wealthy classes of Europe. Marco Polo travelled to China and carried aromatic spices on his return to Europe. Christopher Colombus and subsequent explorers found potatoes, tomatoes, peppers, squashes and maize. Such produce was greeted with a somewhat lukewarm reception and potatoes and tomatoes were received with suspicion and grave misgivings!

It is only in recent generations that people all over the world have expressed interest in vegetables cultivated in different climates.

Nowadays, of course, we have the option of buying exactly what we want, when we want it. This is a luxury we have come to expect and we are ready to pay the price for international variety. Gluts of vegetables, once common seasonal occurrences when produce was cultivated and marketed on a local scale, are not a feature of modern food stores, but seasons still hold good for home-grown produce.

Unlike storecupboard ingredients, the great characteristic of many vegetables is that they still have natural seasons. So, in addition to taking advantage of the fantastic multi-national displays in cosmopolitan supermarkets, it pays also to buy from local growers who offer freshly harvested produce. I think it is important to enjoy summer vegetables during the season to which they traditionally belong and to savour

peas were among the first vegetables farmed in Thessaly and Macedonia. These legumes would have been enormously important to early societies as they grew easily to provide seeds which were a starchy food, high in protein and which dried well for long storage.

Many of our familiar vegetables were cultivated in historic times: the Egyptians grew onions, garlic, radishes, lettuce and broad beans;

the Greeks and Romans farmed produce which was native to their own countries and they also discovered a wider range of plants thanks to their contact with other cultures.

Not only did the Romans discover the fruits of other lands, but their armies also introduced ingredients to the countries they invaded. In Britain, for example, at the beginning of the first century AD, beans, peas, leeks, parsnips and turnips

Above: Spinach.

winter produce in dishes like wholesome stews and broths that are well suited to cooler weather.

NUTRITION

The total contribution of carbohydrate (starchy) foods and vegetables in a well-balanced diet may not be entirely understood, but the benefits and protective role they play in ensuring good health is widely recognized. Expert opinions agree on the fact that we should eat a high proportion of vegetables in our everyday diets.

Although the nutritional value of vegetables varies according to type, freshness, preparation and cooking method, they are a main source of many vitamins, especially vitamin C.

Some of the B-group vitamins are also found in vegetables, particularly in green vegetables and pulses. Carrots and dark green vegetables also include carotene which is used by the body to manufacture vitamin A. Vegetable oils are a useful source of vitamin E.

Vegetables also contain calcium, iron, potassium and magnesium, as well as some trace elements which are required in small quantities.

Starchy vegetables are an important source of energy-giving carbohydrate and they may include useful quantities of fibre.

In a vegetarian diet, vegetables, particularly beans, pulses and sprouting seeds, also make a valuable contribution to the overall protein intake.

Where specific vegetables are a rich source of nutrients, a note is included under the relevant heading.

Vegetables have the highest nutritional content when they are freshly picked. The vitamin content diminishes with staleness and exposure to sunlight. Use fresh vegetables as soon as possible after purchase and always avoid stale limp specimens. The peel and the layer directly beneath it contain a high concentration of nutrients, so it is best to avoid peeling vegetables or to remove the thinnest layer for maximum nutrient retention.

Minerals and vitamins C and B are water soluble and they are lost by seepage into cooking water or the liquid over which vegetables are steamed. To minimize loss of nutrients, do not cut up vegetables finely as this creates a greater surface area for seepage. Vitamin C is also destroyed by long cooking and by exposure to alkalines.

Raw and lightly cooked vegetables provide the best nutritional value and source of fibre. Any cooking liquid should, whenever possible, be used in stocks, gravies or sauces.

ABOUT THIS BOOK

Vegetables can play a starring role in a recipe or they may be combined with other ingredients in a harmony of flavours. Some of the best vegetable soups are examples of well-tuned mixtures - minestrone, for instance, is a blend of onions, carrots, tomatoes and cabbage; or a good old-fashioned vegetable soup brings together simple ingredients such as carrots, turnips and leeks. These, and many others, are loved for the sum of their parts rather than for the taste of individual vegetables.

In general, however, in this book you will find recipes which make the most of each vegetable, so that their particular virtues can be appreciated to the full.

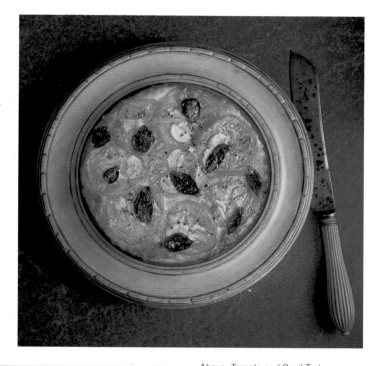

Above: Tomato and Basil Tart.
Left: Red, orange and green peppers.

This is not a vegetarian book; however, there are plenty of recipes which are vegetarian. In many instances, substituting vegetable stock for chicken stock will ensure that the recipe is acceptable.

The recipes are an eclectic mix of classic dishes from around the world and others I have devised over years of cooking; many are perennial favourites with my friends and family. The great thing about cooking with vegetables is, however, that once you have got the hang of using them, a recipe becomes unnecessary. You will discover how you most enjoy carrots, asparagus or less-common vegetables and will learn, as I have, to experiment in your own way. Good Luck!

ONE

ONIONS
AND
LEEKS

Onions

Shallots

Chives

Garlic

Leeks

ONIONS

There are bound to be vegetables you like better than others but a cook would be lost without onions. There are many classic recipes specifically for onion dishes so they can be appreciated in their own right. Onion tarts or French onion soup, for instance, have a sublime flavour and only onions are appropriate. But also, there is hardly a recipe where onions, or their cousins – garlic, leeks or shallots – are not used. Gently fried until soft, or fried more fiercely until golden brown, they add a unique, savoury flavour to dishes.

History

Onions, along with shallots, leeks, chives and garlic, belong to the *Allium* family which, including wild varieties, has some 325 members. All have the characteristic onion smell which is caused by volatile acids beneath the skin.

Archaeological and historical records show that onions have been eaten for thousands of years. They are believed to have originally come from the Middle East and their easy cultivation suggests that their use spread quickly. There are references to the onion in the Bible and it was widely eaten in Egypt. There was, we are told, an inscription on the Great Pyramid stating that the slaves who built the tomb ate their way through 1,600 talents worth of onions, radishes and garlic – presumably a lot, given that the Great Pyramid was made using more than two million 2½-tonne blocks of stone.

By the Middle Ages, onions were a common vegetable throughout Europe and would have been used in soups, stews and sauces when strong flavouring was preferred.

Varieties

As they keep well in a cool place, most people keep a handy stock of onions, usually a general purpose type that can be sautéed or browned. However, onions come in a variety of different colours and strengths, and for certain recipes particular onions are needed.

Right: Spanish onions.
Far right top: Yellow onions.
Far right below: Red onions.

Spanish Onions: Onions raised in warm areas are milder in taste than onions from cooler regions, and Spanish onions are among the mildest cultivated onions. They are a beautiful pale copper colour and are noticeably larger than yellow onions. They have a delicate, sweet flavour which makes them ideal for serving raw in salads, thinly sliced, while their size makes them suitable for stuffing and baking whole.

Yellow Onions: These are the widely available onions you find everywhere and, though called yellow onions, their skins are more golden brown. They are the most pungent of all the onions and are a good, all-purpose variety. The smallest ones, referred to as baby, button or pickling onions, are excellent for pickling but can also be added whole to a casserole or sautéed in butter to make a delicious vegetable accompaniment.

Red Onions: Sometimes called Italian onions, these mild onions have an attractive appearance and are now widely available from most good greengrocers and supermarkets. Below their ruby red skins the flesh is blushed with red. They have a mild, sweet flavour and are excellent thinly sliced and used raw in salads and *antipasti* dishes.

White Onions: These come in all sorts of interesting shapes and sizes – squat, round and oval, big and small. The very small white onions, with shimmery silver skins, are mild and best added whole to stews or served in a creamy sauce. Larger white onions can be mild or strong – there is no way of telling. Like yellow onions, white onions are extremely versatile whether used raw or cooked. The very small white onions, called Paris Silverskin, are the ones used for dry martinis and for commercial pickling.

Vidalia Onions: These popular American onions are a speciality of and named after a town in Georgia, USA. They are a large, pale yellow onion and are deliciously sweet and juicy. Used in salads, or roasted with meat or with other vegetables, they are superb.

Bermuda Onions: These are similar in size to Spanish onions but are rather more squat. They have a mild flavour and are good thinly sliced, fried until golden and served with steaks or burgers.

remove the next layer of onion, as it is often dry or damaged. Unless slicing onions for stir-fries, for which it is customary to slice the onion into wedges, always slice the onion through the rings, widthways. Make whole rings, or for half-rings, cut in half lengthways through the root before slicing (*below*). For finely chopped onion, slice again lengthways.

Spring Onions or Scallions: These are also true onions but harvested very young while their shoots are still green and fresh. They have a mild, delicate taste and both the small white bulb and the green tops can be used in salads, omelettes and stir-fries, or indeed any dish which requires a mild onion flavour.

Nutrition

As well as tasting good, onions are good for you. They contain vitamins B and C together with calcium, iron and potassium. Like garlic, they also contain cycloallin, an anticoagulant which helps protect against heart disease.

Buying and Storing

It used to be a common sight to see an onion seller travelling around the streets on a bicycle with strings of onions hanging from every available support including his own neck.

Nowadays strings of onions are hard to come by although, if you do find them in shops, they are a good way of buying and

storing the vegetable.

Onions, more than almost any other vegetable, keep well provided they are stored in a cool, dry place, such as a larder or outhouse. Do not store them in the fridge as they will go soft, and never keep cut onions in the fridge – or anywhere else – unless you want onion-flavoured milk and an onion-scented home. Onions do not keep well once cut and it is worth buying onions in assorted sizes so that you do not end up having bits left over. Unused bits of onion can be added to stocks; otherwise throw them away.

Preparing

Onions contain a substance which is released when they are cut and causes the eyes to water, quite painfully sometimes. There are all sorts of ways which are supposed to prevent this, including cutting onions under running water, holding a piece of bread between your teeth or wearing goggles!

As well as the outer brown leaves,

Cooking

The volatile acids in onions are driven off during cooking, which is why cooked onion is never as strong as raw onion. The method of cooking, even the way of frying an onion, affects its eventual taste. Boiled onion or chopped onion added neat to soups or casseroles has a stronger, more raw taste. Frying or sautéing briefly, or sweating (frying in a little fat with the lid on) until soft and translucent gives a mild flavour. When fried until golden brown, onions develop a distinct flavour, both sweet and savoury, that is superb in curries and with grilled meats and is essential for French onion soup.

Above far left: Vidalia onions.
Left: White onions.
Above left: Large and small Spring onions.

SHALLOTS

Shallots are not baby onions but a separate member of the onion family. They have a delicate flavour, less intense than most onions and they also dissolve easily into liquids, which is why they are favoured for sauces. Shallots grow in small, tight clusters so that when you break one open there may be two or three bunched together at the root.

Their size makes them convenient for a recipe where only a little onion is required. Use shallots when only a small amount of onion is needed or when only a fine onion flavour is required. Shallots are a pleasant, if maybe extravagant, alternative to onions, but where recipes specify shallots (especially sauce recipes), they should be used if possible.

Although classic cookery frequently calls for particular ingredients, the art of improvisation should not be ignored. For instance, Coq au Vin is traditionally made with walnut-size white onions, but when substituted with shallots, the result is delightful.

History

Shallots are probably as ancient as onions. Roman commentators wrote eloquently about the excellence of shallots in sauces.

Varieties

Shallots are small slender onions with long necks and golden, copper-coloured skins. There are a number of varieties, although there is unlikely to be a choice in the supermarkets. In any case, differences are more in size and colour of skin than in flavour.

Buying and Storing

Like onions, shallots should be firm without any green shoots. They will keep well for several months in a cool dry place.

Preparing and Cooking

Skin shallots in the same way as onions, i.e. top and tail them and then peel off the outer skin. Pull apart the bulbs. Slice them carefully and thinly using a sharp knife – shallots are so small, it is easy to slip and cut yourself. When cooking them whole, fry over a very gentle heat without browning too much.

CHIVES

Chives: In culinary terms, chives are really classed as a herb, but as members of the onion family they are worth mentioning here. As anyone who has grown them knows, chives are tufts of aromatic grass with pretty pale lilac flowers, which are also edible.

Preparing and Serving

Chives are often snipped with scissors and added to egg dishes, or used as a garnish for salads and soups, adding a pleasant but faint onion flavour. Along with parsley, tarragon and chervil, they are an essential ingredient of *fines herbes*.

Chives are also a delicious addition to soft cheeses – far nicer than commercially bought cheeses, where the flavour of chives virtually disappears. Stir also into soft butter for an alternative to garlic butter. This can then be spread on to bread and baked like garlic bread.

If adding to cooked dishes, cook only very briefly, otherwise their flavour will be lost.

Chinese Chives: Chinese chives, sometimes called garlic chives, have a delicate garlic flavour, and if you see them for sale in your local Chinese supermarket, they are worth buying as they add a delicate onion flavour to stir-fries and other oriental dishes.

Preparing and Serving

Use them as you would chives - both the green and white parts are edible. They are also delicious served on their own as a vegetable accompaniment.

Buying and Storing

For both types of chives, look for plump, uniformly green specimens with no brown spots or signs of wilting. They can be stored for up to a week in the fridge. Unopened flowers on Chinese chives are an indication that the plant is young and therefore more tender than one with fully opened flowers.

Above left: Chives.
Above right: Chinese chives.

GARLIC

Garlic is an ingredient that almost anyone who does any cooking at all, and absolutely everyone who enjoys cooking, would not be without.

History

Garlic is known to have been first grown in around 3200 BC. Inscriptions and models of garlic found in the pyramids of ancient Egypt testify to the fact that garlic was not only an important foodstuff but that it had ceremonial significance as well. The Greeks and Romans likewise believed garlic to have magical qualities. Warriors would eat it for strength before going into battle, gods were appeased with gifts of garlic, and cloves of garlic were fastened round the necks of babies to ward off evil. Hence, vampire mythology has ancient precedents.

The Greeks and Romans also used garlic for its therapeutic qualities. Not only was it thought to be an aphrodisiac but also it was believed to be good for eczema, toothache and snake bites.

Although garlic found its way all over Europe – vats of butter, strongly flavoured with garlic, have been found by archaeologists working in Ireland which date back 200-300 years – fundamentally, its popularity today derives from our liking for Mediterranean, Indian and Asian food, in which garlic plays a very important part.

Nutrition

As is often the case, what was once dismissed as an old wives' tale is, after thorough scientific inquiry, found to be true. Garlic is a case in point; most authorities accept that it has many therapeutic properties. The most significant of these is that it lowers blood cholesterol, thus helping prevent heart disease. Also, raw garlic contains a powerful antibiotic and there is evidence that it has a beneficial effect against cancer and strokes, and increases the absorption of vitamins. Many garlic enthusiasts take their garlic in tablet form, but true devotees prefer to take it as it comes.

Right: A string of pink-skinned garlic.

Varieties

There are numerous varieties of garlic, from the large "elephant" garlic, to small tight bulbs. Their papery skin can be white, pink or purple. Colour makes no difference to taste but the particular attraction of the large purple bulbs is that they make a beautiful display in the kitchen.

As a general rule, the smaller the garlic bulb, the stronger it is likely to be. However, most garlic sold in shops is not classified in either shape or form (unless it is elephant garlic) and in practice you will simply pick up whatever you need, either loose, in bunches or on strings.

Garlic grown in a hot climate is likely to be the most pungent, and fresh new season's garlic has a subtle, mild flavour that is particularly good if it is to be used raw, for example, in salads and for dressings.

Above: Elephant garlic beside normal-size bulbs.

Buying and Storing

Garlic bulbs should be firm and round with clear, papery skins. Avoid any that are beginning to sprout. Garlic bulbs keep well stored in a cool, dry place; if the air is damp they will sprout and if it is too warm the cloves will eventually turn to grey powder.

Preparing and Cooking

First break the garlic bulb into cloves and then remove the papery skin. You can blanch this off with hot water but using a fingernail or knife is just as effective. When a garlic clove is split lengthways a shoot is revealed in the centre, which is occasionally green, and some people remove this whatever the colour. Cloves are the little segments which make up the bulb and most recipes call for one or more cloves of garlic. (Don't use a bulb when you just need a clove!)

Crush cloves either with the blade of a knife or use a garlic crusher. Crushed garlic cooks more evenly and distributes its flavour in food better than when it is used sliced or finely chopped (stir-fries are the exception). Prepare garlic according to the strength of flavour required: thinly sliced garlic is milder than chopped, which in turn is milder than crushed garlic and, of course, cooking mutes the pungency.

Garlic Breath

The taste and smell of garlic tends to linger on the breath and can be a problem to get rid of. Chewing parsley is a well-known remedy but is only moderately successful. Chewing the seeds of cardamom pods is also said to work but is rather unpleasant. The best suggestion is to eat garlic with your friends so that nobody notices!

LEEKS

Leeks are very versatile, having their own distinct, subtle flavour. They are excellent in pies and casseroles with other ingredients, braised in cream and served by themselves, or simmered in butter as an accompanying vegetable.

Leeks are also wonderful in soups and broths and have rightly earned the title, "king of the soup onions". Cock-a-leekie from Scotland and *Crème Vichyssoise*, invented by the chef of New York's Ritz-Carlton, are two classic leek soups, but many other soups call for leeks.

History

Leeks, like onions and garlic, have a long history. They were grown widely in ancient Egypt and were also eaten and enjoyed throughout the Greek and Roman period. In England, there is evidence that leeks were enjoyed during the Dark Ages. There is little mention of them during the Middle Ages, and history suggests that between the sixteenth and eighteenth centuries eating leeks was not considered fashionable.

However, while they may not have enjoyed a good reputation among the notoriously fickle aristocracy, the rural communities probably continued to eat leeks. They grow in all sorts of climates and are substantial enough to make a reasonable meal for a poor family. It was probably during this time that they were dubbed "poor man's asparagus" – a name which says more about people's snobbery about food than it does about leeks.

Many place names in England, such as Leckhampstead and Leighton Buzzard are derived from the word leek and, of course, the leek has been a national emblem of Wales for hundreds of years.

Varieties

There are many different varieties of leeks but among them there is little difference in flavour. Commercially grown leeks tend to be about 25cm/10in long and about 2cm/³/4in in diameter. Leeks nurtured in home gardens can be left to grow to an enormous size but these may develop a woody centre.

RAMP

Among the many wild onions and leeks, the Canadian ramp is perhaps the best known. Also called the wild leek, it looks a little like a spring onion, but has a stronger and more assertive garlic-onion flavour. Choose unblemished, clear white specimens with bright, fresh leaves and keep in a cool place, wrapped in a plastic bag to store.

Prepare and cook as you would spring onions, by trimming the root end and then slicing thinly. Use in cooking or in salads but remember the onion flavour is stronger, so use sparingly.

Buying and Storing

Buy leeks which look fresh and healthy. The white part should be firm and unblemished and the leaves green and lively. As leeks do not keep particularly well, it is best to buy them as and when you need them. If you need to store them, trim away the top of the leaves and keep them in the salad drawer of the fridge or in a cool place. After several days they will begin to shrivel.

Preparing

It is important to wash leeks thoroughly before cooking as earth and grit lodges itself between the white sections at the base. To prepare leeks, cut away the flags (leaves) and trim the base. Unless the leek is extremely fresh or home grown, you will probably have to remove the first layer of white; then cut a slit from one end to the other through to the centre of the leek *(below)*. Wash under cold running water, pulling the sections apart so that the water rinses out any stubborn pieces of earth. If you slice the leeks – either slice thickly or thinly – place them in a colander and rinse thoroughly under cold water.

Cooking

Leeks can be steamed or boiled and then added to your recipe, or fry sliced leeks gently in butter for a minute or so and then cover with a lid to sweat so they cook without browning. Unlike onions, leeks shouldn't be allowed to brown; they become tough and unappetizing. They can be stir-fried, however, with a little garlic and ginger. If they begin to cook too fiercely, splash in a little stock and soy sauce and simmer until tender.

Left: Leeks.
Above: Ramp.

TWO

SHOOTS
AND
STEMS

Asparagus

Globe Artichokes

Celery

Celeriac

Fiddlehead Fern

Oriental Shoots

Fennel

Samphire

ASPARAGUS

Asparagus is definitely a luxury vegetable. Its price, even in season, sets it apart from cabbages and cauliflowers, and it has a taste of luxury too. The spears, especially the thick, green spears, at their best in early summer, have an intense, rich flavour that is impossible to describe but easy to remember. If the gods eat, they will eat asparagus – served simply with a good Hollandaise!

History

The ancient Greeks enjoyed wild asparagus but it was not until the Roman period that we know it was cultivated. Even then asparagus was highly thought of; it is recorded that Julius Caesar liked to eat it with melted butter. There is little mention of asparagus being eaten in England until the seventeenth century. Mrs Beeton has 14 recipes for asparagus and from the prices quoted in her cookbook it is apparent that it was expensive even in Victorian times.

Nutrition

Asparagus provides vitamins A, B2 and C and is also a good source of potassium, iron and calcium. It is a well-known diuretic.

Varieties

There are many varieties of asparagus and many different ways of raising it too. Spanish and some Dutch asparagus is white with ivory tips; it is grown under mounds of soil and cut just as the tips begin to show. The purple variety is mostly grown in France, where the spears are cut once the tips are about 4cm/1 1/2 in above the ground. Consequently, the stalks are white and the tops tinged with green or purple. In contrast, English and American asparagus grows above the ground and the spears are entirely green. Arguments continue over which has the better flavour, most growers expressing a preference for their own asparagus!

 Thin, short asparagus are called sprue and are excellent when briefly steamed or stir-fried and added to salads. In Italy, they are served by themselves, scattered with grated Parmesan cheese.

Preparing

Unless the asparagus comes straight from the garden, cut off the bottom of the stalk as it is usually hard and woody. If the bottom parts of the stem also feel hard, pare this away with a potato peeler *(below)*. However, if the asparagus is very fresh, this is not necessary, and sprue rarely needs trimming at all.

Buying and Storing

Asparagus has a relatively short growing season from late spring to early summer. Nowadays, it is available in the shops almost all year round but outside the season it will have been imported. It is still good, but it is expensive and will not have the flavour of home-produced asparagus, since it starts to lose its flavour once it is cut.

When buying asparagus, the tips should be tightly furled and fresh looking, and the stalks fresh and straight. If the stalks are badly scarred or droopy, it indicates that they have been hanging around for too long and it is not worth buying. Asparagus will keep for several days if necessary. Untie the bundles and store in the salad drawer of the fridge.

Cooking

The problem with cooking asparagus is that the stalks take longer to cook than the tender tips, which need to be only briefly steamed. Ideally, use an asparagus kettle. Place the asparagus spears with the tips upwards in the wire basket and then lower into a little boiling salted water in the kettle. Cover and cook until the stems are tender.

Alternatively, if you don't have an asparagus kettle, place the bundle upright in a deep saucepan of boiling salted water. (The bundle can be wedged into place with potatoes.) Cover with a dome of foil and cook for 5-10 minutes or until the spears are tender. The cooking time depends largely on the thickness of the spears but take care not to overcook; the spears should still have a "bite" to them.

Asparagus can also be roasted in a little olive oil. This cooking method intensifies the flavour and is gratifyingly simple. Serve with just a sprinkling of sea salt – it's quite delicious! If steaming asparagus, serve simply with melted butter, which perfectly complements the luxury of the vegetable.

Left: Asparagus.
Above: White asparagus.

GLOBE ARTICHOKES

Globe artichokes have an exquisite flavour and are a very sociable food to eat. They grow in abundance in Brittany, and during July and August farmers can frequently be seen selling them by the roadside. The globes are huge hearty specimens and are extremely fresh, so they make a good buy.

History

It is not known for certain whether artichokes were eaten in antiquity. Although they are mentioned by writers, they could have been referring to the cardoon, which is the uncultivated form of artichoke. Cardoons grew wild in many southern European countries, and, as far as we know, cultivated artichokes first became a popular food in Italy. However, Goethe did not share the Italians' liking for the vegetable and remarks in his book, *Travels Through Italy*, that "the peasants eat thistles", something he didn't care for at all.

Nowadays, artichokes are grown all over southern Europe and in California. People in Italy, France and Spain eat artichokes while the vegetable is still young, before the choke has formed and the entire artichoke is edible. Unfortunately, such young delicacies are not exported but look out for them if you are in these countries.

Buying and Storing

It is only worth buying artichokes when they are in season, although they are available in supermarkets almost all year round. In winter, however, they are sad looking specimens, small and rather dry, and are really not worth the bother of cooking. At their best, artichokes should be lively looking with a good bloom on their leaves, the inner leaves wrapped tightly round the choke and heart inside. Artichokes will keep for 2-3 days in the salad drawer of the fridge but are best eaten as soon as possible.

Preparing and Cooking

First twist off the stalk which should also remove some of the fibres at the base and then cut the base flat and pull away any small base leaves. If the leaves are very spiky, trim them with a pair of scissors if liked *(above)*, then rinse under running water. Cook in boiling water, acidulated with the juice of half a lemon. Large artichokes need to be simmered for 30-40 minutes until tender. To test if they are done, pull off one of the outer leaves. It should come away easily and the base of the leaf should be tender.

prickly choke and discard, to reveal the heart. Eat the heart with a knife and fork, dipping it in the garlic butter or vinaigrette.

CARDOONS

This impressively large vegetable is closely related to the globe artichoke and has a superb flavour, a cross between artichokes and asparagus. Cultivated plants frequently grow to 2 metres/6 feet in height, and once mature, cardoons, like celery, are blanched as they grow. This process involves wrapping the stalks with newspaper and black bags for several weeks, so that when harvested, in late autumn, before the frosts, the stalks are a pale green.

The cardoon is a popular vegetable in southern Europe but less commonly available elsewhere. In Spain, for instance, it is much appreciated and often appears on the table, poached and served with chestnuts or walnuts. Only the inner ribs and heart are used.

Artichokes and Drink

Artichokes contain a chemical called cynarin, which in many people (although surprisingly not all) affects the taste buds by enhancing sweet flavours. Among other things, this will spoil the taste of wine. Consequently, don't waste good wine with artichokes but drink iced water instead, which should taste pleasantly sweet.

Eating Artichokes

Artichokes are fun to eat. They have to be eaten with fingers, which does away with any pomp and ceremony, always a handicap for a good dinner party. Serve one artichoke between two, so that people can share the fun of pulling off the leaves and dipping them into garlic butter or vinaigrette. If you want to serve one each, serve them in succession. The dipping sauces are an essential part of eating artichokes; people can either spoon a little on to their plates or give everyone a little bowl each. After dipping, draw the leaf through your teeth, eating the fleshy part and piling the

remains of the leaf on your plate. When most of the leaves have been eaten, a few thin pointed leaves remain in the centre, which can be pulled off altogether. Then pull or cut away the fine

Far left: Globe artichokes.
Top: Baby globe artichokes.
Above: Cardoons.

CELERY

Some people say that the very act of eating celery has a slimming effect because chewing it uses up more calories than the vegetable itself contains. Although it may be insubstantial, celery nevertheless has a distinct and individual flavour, sharp and savoury, which makes it an excellent flavouring for soups and stuffings, as well as good on its own or in salads. The astringent flavour and crunchy texture of celery contrasts well with the other ingredients in salads such as Waldorf salad or walnut and avocado salad.

History

Celery has been eaten in this country for several hundred years, having been introduced from Italy where it was commonly eaten in salads.

Nutrition

Celery is very low in calories but contains potassium and calcium.

Varieties

Most greengrocers and supermarkets, depending on the time of year, sell both green and white celery and you would be excused for not knowing the difference. When celery is allowed to grow naturally, the stalks are green. However, by banking up earth against the shoots celery is blanched: the stalks are protected from sunlight and remain pale and white. Consequently, white celery is often "dirty" – covered loosely in soil – while green celery will always be clean. White celery, which is frost hardy, is only available in winter. It is more tender and less bitter than green celery and is generally considered superior. Celery is therefore thought of as a winter vegetable and is traditionally used at Christmas time, for stuffing and as a sauce to go with turkey or ham.

Buying and Storing

White celery is in season during the winter months. If possible, buy "dirty" celery which hasn't been washed. It has a better flavour than the pristine but rather bland supermarket variety. Look for celery with green fresh-looking leaves and straight stems. If the leaves or any outer stalks are missing, it is likely to be rather old, so worth avoiding.

Celery will keep for several days in the salad drawer of the refrigerator. Limp celery can be revived by wrapping it in absorbent paper and standing it in a jar of water.

Preparing

Wash if necessary and pull the stalks apart, trimming the base with a sharp knife. Cut into thick or thin slices according to the recipe. When served raw and whole, the coarse outer "strings" should be removed from each stalk by pulling them up from the base.

Cooking and Serving

Serve celery raw and finely sliced in salads, mixed with cream cheese or soured cream. Braised celery is tasty, either whole or sliced. Celery has a distinctive, savoury, astringent flavour so is excellent in soups or stuffings.

CELERIAC

Strictly speaking, celeriac is a root vegetable, being the root of certain kinds of celery. It is knobbly with a patchy brown/white skin and has a similar but less pronounced flavour than celery. Grated and eaten raw, it has a crunchy texture, but when cooked it is more akin to potatoes. Thin slices of potato and celeriac cooked *au gratin* with cream is a popular way of serving this vegetable.

Buying and Preparing

If possible, buy smallish bulbs of celeriac. The flesh discolours when exposed to light, so as soon as you have peeled, sliced, diced or grated the celeriac, plunge it into a bowl of acidulated water (water with lemon juice added).

Cooking

Celeriac can be used in soups and broths, or can be diced and boiled and eaten in potato salads.

Left: Green celery.
Above: White celery.
Right: Celeriac.

FIDDLEHEAD FERN

Sometimes called the ostrich fern, these shoots are a rich green colour and are normally about 5cm/2in long. They have an unusual flavour, something like a cross between asparagus and okra, and have a slightly chewy texture, which makes them a popular choice for oriental dishes.

Preparing and Cooking

To prepare and cook, trim the ends and then steam or simmer in a little water or sauté in butter until tender. Use in salads or serve as a first course with a Hollandaise sauce.

Right: Fiddlehead ferns.
Below left: Alfalfa sprouts.
Below right: Mung bean sprouts.

ORIENTAL SHOOTS

BAMBOO SHOOTS

In the Far East, edible bamboo shoots are sold fresh in the market. The young shoots are stripped of their brown outer skins and the insides are then eaten. Although fresh bamboo shoots can occasionally be found in oriental stores, the most readily available variety is sold in cans. The flavour is undoubtedly spoilt. Fresh bamboo shoots have a mild but distinct taste, faintly reminiscent of globe artichokes, while canned ones really taste of nothing at all. However, the texture, which, in Chinese cuisines particularly, is as important as the flavour, is not so impaired, and bamboo shoots have a pleasantly crunchy bite.

Preparing and Cooking

Peel away the outer skin and then cook in boiling water for about half an hour. They should feel firm, but not "rock" hard. Once cooked, slice thinly and serve by themselves as a side dish, with garlic butter or a sauce, or add to stir-fries, spring rolls or any oriental dish

where you need a contrast of textures. Since canned bamboo shoots have been preserved in brine, always rinse well before using.

BEAN SPROUTS

Bean sprouts are rather a neglected vegetable, used almost carelessly for orien-

tal dishes but otherwise passed by as being insipid and not very interesting. It's a reputation they don't deserve: not only do they have a lovely fresh flavour, but they are also good for you.

All sorts of seeds can be sprouted, but the bean family are favourites among the sprouted vegetables. The bean sprouts most commonly available in the shops are sprouted mung beans, but aduki beans, alfalfa, lentils and soybeans can all be sprouted and taste delicious.

Nutrition

Beans sprouts contain a significant amount of protein, Vitamin C and many of the B vitamins. They have an excellent flavour too, best appreciated eaten raw in salads or sandwiches, and for slimmers they are an ideal food, low in calories, yet with sufficient substance to be filling, and with a flavour and texture that can be enjoyed without a dressing.

Buying and Storing

Bean sprouts should only be bought when absolutely fresh. They don't keep for long and they will taste sour if past their best. The sprouts should be firm, not limp, and and the tips should be green or yellow; avoid any that are beginning to turn brown.

Cooking

If stir-frying, add the bean sprouts at the last minute so they cook for the minimum period to keep plenty of crunch and retain their nutritional value. Most health food shops will have instructions on sprouting your own beans. Only buy seeds intended for sprouting.

PALM HEARTS

Fresh palm hearts are the buds of cabbage palm trees and are considered a delicacy in many parts of the world. They are available canned from oriental stores, but are most prized when fresh. These should be blanched before being cooked to eliminate any bitterness. They can be braised or sautéed and then served hot with a Hollandaise sauce, or cold with a simple vinaigrette.

WATER CHESTNUTS

Water chestnut is the common name for a number of aquatic herbs and their nut-like fruit, the best known and most popular variety being the Chinese water chestnut, sometimes known as the Chinese sedge. In China they are grown in exactly the same way as rice, the plants needing the same conditions of

high temperatures, shallow water and good soil. In spring, the corms are planted in paddy fields which are then flooded to a depth of some 10cm/4in. These are drained in autumn, and the corms are harvested and stored over the winter. Water chestnuts are much used in Chinese cooking and have a sweet crunchy flavour with nutty overtones.

They are edible cooked or raw and are excellent in all sorts of Chinese dishes.

Above: Sprouting mung beans.
Below: clockwise from top left: Canned Water chestnuts, canned Bamboo shoots, fresh Water chestnuts, canned Palm hearts.

FENNEL

The vegetable fennel is closely related to the herb and spice of the same name. It is called variously Florence fennel, sweet fennel, *finocchio dulce* or Italian fennel.

Like the herb, Florence fennel has the distinct flavour of anise, a taste that seems to go particularly well with fish, so the vegetable is often served with fish dishes while the herb or spice is commonly used in fish stocks, sauces or soups. The leaves are edible and can be used in soups and stocks as well as for garnishing.

History

Florence fennel has only been popular in Britain for the last 20 years, although it has a long history of cultivation, having been eaten by the ancient Egyptians, Greeks and Romans. In Italy, fennel has been eaten for several centuries: many of the best fennel recipes come from Italy and other parts of the Mediterranean.

Buying and Storing

If possible, buy small tender bulbs. The bulbs should be clean and white with no bruises or blemishes and the feathery leaves should be green and lively. Fennel will keep for a day or two in the salad drawer of the fridge.

Preparing

Unless the bulbs are very young and tender, remove the first layer of skin, as it is likely to be tough (this can be used for a stock). Fennel can then be sliced into slivers by cutting downwards or into rings by cutting across the bulb. When used raw in salads, it needs to be cut into smaller pieces.

Cooking and Serving

Fennel can be served raw if it is thinly sliced and dressed with a light vinaigrette. In salads, its flavour contrasts well with apple, celery and other crunchy ingredients. Fennel is also excellent braised with onions, tomatoes and garlic.

Right: Florence fennel.
Far right: Marsh samphire.

SAMPHIRE

There are two types of samphire. Marsh samphire grows in estuaries and salt marshes while rock samphire, sometimes called sea fennel, grows on rocky shores. The two are understandably confused since they are both connected with the sea, yet they are completely different plants.

The type likely to be sold by a fishmonger is marsh samphire. It is also known as glasswort and is sometimes called sea asparagus, as its shoots are similar to sprue, small asparagus shoots.

Although marsh samphire grows easily and is commonly found all over Europe and North America, it is not cultivated and is only available for a short time while it is in season, normally in late summer and early autumn.

Samphire has a distinctly salty, iodine flavour and a pleasant crisp texture. The flavour is reminiscent of the sea and goes particularly well with fish and seafood. However, samphire can be enjoyed simply steamed and dipped into melted butter.

Buying and Storing

When in season, good fishmongers get regular stocks of marsh samphire, and it should look bright and fresh. Buy it as you need it, as it will not keep for long.

Preparing and Cooking

If necessary, wash marsh samphire under cold running water. It is best steamed over a pan of boiling water for no more than 3 minutes. Alternatively, blanch it in boiling water for 3-5 minutes and then drain. Samphire can be eaten raw but blanching it removes some of the saltiness.

To eat samphire, draw the shoots through the teeth to peel the succulent part from the thin central core.

ROOTS

POTATOES

History

The potato originates from South America. Most people learned at school that Sir Walter Raleigh brought the tubers to England from Virginia, but this never convinced historians as the potato was completely unknown in North America until the eighteenth century. They now believe that Sir Francis Drake was responsible. In 1586, after battling against the Spaniards in the Caribbean, Drake stopped to pick up provisions from Cartegena in northern Colombia – and these included tobacco and potato tubers. En route home, he stopped off at Roanoke Island, off the coast of Virginia. The first group of English colonists had been sponsored to settle there by Sir Walter Raleigh but by this time they had had enough. Drake brought them back to England, along with some of Raleigh's men and, of course, the provisions – including the potato tubers.

Potatoes apparently fascinated Queen Elizabeth and intrigued horticulturists, but they were not an overnight success among the people. The wealthy frequently reviled them as being flavourless and the food of the poor. People distrusted the fact that they reached maturity underground, believing them to be the work of

the devil. In Scotland, Presbyterian ministers darkly advised their congregations that there was no mention of potatoes in the Bible, and thus the eating of them was an ungodly act!

In spite of such a bad press, potatoes nevertheless were slowly recognized for their merit. By 1650 they were the staple food of Ireland, and elsewhere in Europe potatoes began to replace wheat as the most important crop, both for people and for livestock. In an early English cookery book, *Adam's Luxury and Eve's Cookery*, there are 20 different recipes for cooking and serving potatoes.

The first mention of potatoes in America is in 1719 in Londonderry, New Hampshire. They arrived not from the south, but via Irish settlers who brought their potatoes with them.

The current popularity of potatoes is probably thanks to a Frenchman called Antoine-Auguste Parmentier. A military pharmacist of the latter part of the eighteenth century, Parmentier recognized the virtues of the potato, both for its versatility and as an important food for the poor, and set out to improve its image. He persuaded Louis XVI to let him ostentatiously grow potatoes on royal land around the palace in Versailles to

impress the fashion-conscious Parisians. He also produced a court dinner in which each course contained potatoes. Gradually, eating potatoes became chic, first among people in the French court and then in French Society. Today, if you see *Parmentier* in a recipe or on a menu, it means "with potato".

Nutrition

Potatoes are an important source of carbohydrate. Once thought to be fattening, we now know that, on the contrary, potatoes can be an excellent part of a calorie-controlled diet – provided, of course, they are not fried in oil or mashed with too much butter. Potatoes are also a very good source of vitamin C, and during the winter potatoes are often the main source of this vitamin. They also contain potassium, iron and vitamin B.

Varieties

There are more than 400 varieties of potato but unless you are a gardener, you will find only some 15 varieties generally available. Thanks to labelling laws, packaged potatoes carry their names which makes it easier to learn to differentiate between the varieties and find out which potato is good for what.

New Potatoes

Carlingford: Available as a new potato or as main crop, Carlingford has a close white flesh.
Jersey Royal: Often the first new potato of the season, Jersey Royals have been shipped from Jersey for over a hundred years and have acquired an enviable reputation among everyone who enjoys good food. Boiled or steamed and then served with butter and a sprinkling of parsley, they cannot be beaten.

Jersey Royals are kidney-shaped, with yellow firm flesh and a distinctive flavour. Don't confuse Jersey Royals with Jersey Whites, which are actually Maris Pipers, grown in Jersey.
Maris Bard: A regularly shaped, slightly waxy potato with white flesh.
Maris Peer: This variety has dry firm flesh and a waxy texture and doesn't disintegrate when cooked – consequently, it is good in salads.

Main Crop Potatoes

Desirée: A potato with a pink skin and yellow soft-textured flesh. It is good for baking, chipping, roasting and mashing.

Estima: A good all-rounder with yellow flesh and pale skin.

Golden Wonder: A russet-skinned potato that was the original favourite for making crisps. It has an excellent, distinctive flavour, and should you find them for sale, buy them at once for baked potatoes. They are also good boiled or roasted.

Kerr's Pink: A good cooking potato with pink skin and creamy flesh.

King Edward: Probably the best known of British potatoes, although not the best in flavour. King Edwards are creamy white in colour with a slightly floury texture.

Red King Edwards are virtually identical except for their red skin. Both are good roasted or baked. However, the flesh disintegrates when boiled, so while good for mashing do not use King Edwards if you want whole boiled potatoes.

Maris Piper: This is a widely grown variety of potato, popular with growers and cooks because it is good for all kinds of cooking methods – baking, chipping, roasting and mashing. It has a pale, smooth skin and creamy white flesh.

Left: Maris Bard potatoes.
Above: Kerr's pink (left) and Maris Piper (right) potatoes.
Right: Romano potatoes.

Pentland Dell: A long, oval-shaped potato with a floury texture that tends to disintegrate when boiled. For this reason, it is popular for roasting as the outside becomes soft when par-boiled and then crisps up with the fat during roasting.

Romano: The Romano has a distinctive red skin with creamy flesh and is a good all-rounder, similar to Desirée.

Wilja: Introduced from Holland, this is a pale, yellow-fleshed potato with a good, sweet flavour and waxy texture.

Other Varieties

Although most of these varieties are also main crop, they are less widely available than those listed above but are increasingly sold in supermarkets. They are recommended for salads but many are also excellent sautéed or simply boiled.

Cara: A large main crop potato, which is excellent baked or boiled but is a good all-rounder.

Finger Potatoes: Thumb-sized, long baby potatoes are sometimes called finger potatoes or fingerlings. Among the many varieties are the German Lady's Finger. Since they are new crop potatoes, they need simply be boiled and then served either in salads or with a little butter and a sprinkling of parsley.

La Ratte: A French potato with a smooth skin and waxy yellow flesh. It has a chestnut flavour and is good in salads.

Linzer Delikatess: These small, kidney-shaped potatoes look a little like Jersey Royals but have a pale smooth skin. They do not have much taste and are best in salads where their flavour can be enhanced with other ingredients.

Pink Fir Apple: This is an old English variety, with pink skin and a smooth yellow flesh. It is becoming increasingly popular and has a distinctive flavour.

Above left: Cara (left) and Estima (right) potatoes.
Left: Linzer Delikatess potatoes.
Above: Desirée (left) and King Edward (right) potatoes.
Right: Finger potatoes.

Purple Congo: If you want to startle your friends, serve some of these striking purple-blue potatoes. There are several varieties of blue potato, ranging from a pale lavender to a purple-black, but one of the most popular is the Purple Congo, which is a wonderful deep purple. They are best boiled and served simply with a little butter and do retain their colour when cooked.

Truffe de Chine: Another deep purple, almost black potato, of unknown origin but now grown in France. It has a nutty, slightly mealy flavour and is best served in a salad with a simple dressing. Like the Purple Congo, it retains its colour after being cooked.

Recommended Varieties for Cooking

Baking: As for roasting, use potatoes with a floury texture, such as Golden Wonder, Pentland Dell, King Edward and Maris Piper.

Boiling: Jersey Royal, Maris Bard and Maris Peer, or any of the Egyptian or Belgian new crop varieties. In addition, Pink Fir Apple, La Ratte and Linzer Delikatess are excellent.

Chipping: King Edward, Golden Wonder, Romano, Maris Piper and Desirée.

Mashing: Golden Wonder, Maris Piper, King Edward, Wilja, Romano and Pentland Dell.

Roasting: Pentland Dell, Golden Wonder, Maris Piper, King Edward, Desiree and Romano are among the best roasting potatoes. Ideally, use potatoes with a floury texture.

Salads: All the small, specialist potatoes, such as La Ratte, Pink Fir Apple and Linzer Delikatess as well as Finger Potatoes and small new potatoes.

Sautéing: Any waxy type of potato, such as Maris Bard, Maris Peer, any of the specialist potatoes, and Romano and Maris Piper.

Buying and Storing

Potatoes should always be stored in a dark, cool, dry place. If they are stored exposed to the light, green patches will develop which can be poisonous, and they will go mouldy if kept in the damp. When buying potatoes in bulk, it is best to buy them in paper sacks rather than plastic bags as humid conditions will cause them to go rotten. Similarly, if you buy potatoes in polythene bags, remove them when you get home and place them in a vegetable rack or in a paper bag, in a dark place.

Main crop potatoes will keep for several months in the right conditions but will gradually lose their nutritional value. New potatoes should be eaten within two or three days as they will go mouldy if stored for too long.

Preparing

Most of the minerals and vitamins contained in potatoes are contained in or just below the skin. It is therefore better to eat potatoes in their skins. New potatoes need only be washed under running water; older potatoes need to be scrubbed.

If you peel potatoes, use a peeler that removes only the very top surface (*below left*) or, alternatively, for salads and cold dishes, boil the potatoes in their skins and peel when cool.

Cooking

Baking: Cook baked potatoes in a low oven for well browned and crunchy skins and fluffy flesh. Baked potatoes can be cooked more quickly in a microwave oven; for a crunchy texture to the skin place them in a hot oven for 10 minutes.

Boiling: It is impossible to generalize on how long to boil as it depends so much on the variety of potato. Try to cut potatoes to an even size (new potatoes should not need to be cut), salt the water if liked, cover and cook over a moderate heat. Don't boil potatoes too fiercely; old ones especially may disintegrate and leave you with a pan of starchy water.

Chips: Home-cooked chips are a treat worth occasionally giving the family instead of the convenient but otherwise disappointing oven chips. However, they are fatty and therefore not good for you when eaten in great quantities or too often.

To make them, cut the potatoes into even-size chips and place in a bowl of cold water for about 10 minutes before frying. Drain and then dry in a piece of muslin or an old dish towel before frying. Fry only as many chips as will comfortably sit in the fat. Halfway through cooking, drain them and allow the oil to come back to temperature before plunging the chips back in. This browns the chips and they don't soak up excessive amounts of oil. Be warned; the cooking smells from making chips tend to linger!

Mashing: Boil the potatoes until tender, drain thoroughly and then tip them back into the pan; mash with a little milk and

butter using a potato masher (*below right*), and season to taste with a little salt, if necessary, and pepper. Never use a food processor or liquidizer: the potatoes will turn into an inedible thick grey paste. You may lightly whisk potatoes with a fork after mashing to fluff them up but no more – for once modern machines have not improved on the basic utensil.

Roast Potatoes: The best roast potatoes are made using a floury textured potato such as Maris Piper or King Edward. Wash and cut them into even-size chunks and par-boil them in lightly salted water until they begin to go tender and the outside looks soft. Drain them through a sieve or colander and then tip them back into the saucepan, put the lid on and shake the pan two or three times. This roughens up the surface of the potato. Place the potatoes in a dish of hot oil or fat, or round a joint of meat, and turn them over so that they are evenly coated. Roast them in the oven for 40-50 minutes until golden. Serve as soon as possible once cooked as the outsides become leathery if they are kept in a warm oven for too long.

Sautéing: There are various ways to sauté potatoes and no one way is better than another. For sautéed sliced potatoes, par-boil whole potatoes for 5-10 minutes until they begin to soften. Drain them thoroughly and then slice into thick rounds. Using sunflower oil or a mixture of sunflower and olive oil (not butter as it will burn), fry them in a large frying pan. Turn the potatoes occasionally and cook until evenly browned. For sautéed, diced potatoes, cut the potatoes into small cubes, blanch for 2 minutes and then drain well. Either fry them on the stove or cook them in a little oil in the oven; turn them once or twice to brown evenly.

Steaming: New potatoes are excellent steamed. Place them on a bed of mint in a steamer or a colander over a pan of boiling water for 15-20 minutes.

Above left: Purple Congo potatoes.
Below left: Truffe de Chine (left) and Pink Fir Apple (right) potatoes.

PARSNIPS

There's something very old-fashioned about parsnips. They conjure up images of cold winter evenings and warm comforting broths supped in front of a blazing wood fire. Nowadays parsnips are available all year through, but many people still feel they belong to winter, adding their characteristic flavour to soups and stews.

Parsnips are related to carrots, similarly sweet but with a distinct earthy flavour that blends well with other root vegetables and is also enhanced with spices and garlic.

History

Parsnips have a long history. The Romans grew and cooked them to make broths and stews. When they conquered Gaul and Britain, the Romans discovered that root vegetables grown in northerly areas had a better flavour than those grown in the south – they may have been the first to decree that parsnips should be eaten after the first frost!

Throughout the Dark Ages and early Middle Ages, parsnips were the main starchy vegetable for ordinary people (the potato had yet to be introduced). Parsnips were not only easy to grow but were a welcome food to eat during the lean winter months. They were also valued for their sugar content. Sweet parsnip dishes like jam and desserts became part of traditional English cookery, and they were also commonly used for making beer and wine. Parsnip wine is still one of the most popular of the country wines, with a beautiful golden colour and a rich sherry-like flavour.

Nutrition

Parsnips contain moderate amounts of vitamins A and C, along with some of the B vitamins. They are also a source of calcium, iron and potassium.

Buying and Storing

Parsnips are really a winter crop, although nowadays they are available all year round. Tradition has it that parsnips are best after the first frost, but many people like the very young tender parsnips available in the early summer. When buying parsnips, choose small or

medium-size specimens as the large ones tend to be rather fibrous. They should feel firm and be a pale ivory colour without any sprouting roots. Store parsnips in a cool place, ideally an airy larder or cool outhouse, where they will keep well for 8-10 days.

Preparing

Very small parsnips need little or no peeling; just trim the ends and cook according to your recipe. Medium-size and large parsnips need to be peeled. Larger parsnips also need to have the woody core removed; if it is cut out before cooking, the parsnips will cook more quickly and evenly.

Cooking

Roast parsnips are best par-boiled for a few minutes before adding to the roasting dish. Very young parsnips can be roasted whole but larger ones are best halved or quartered lengthways. Roast in butter or oil for about 40 minutes in an oven preheated to 200°C /400°F /Gas 6.

To boil parsnips, cut them into pieces about 5cm/2in long and boil for 15-20 minutes until tender. When boiled briefly like this, they keep their shape, but when added to a casserole or stew they eventually disintegrate. Don't worry if this happens; parsnips need plenty of cooking so that the flavour can blend with the other ingredients.

JERUSALEM ARTICHOKES

Jerusalem artichokes are related to the sunflower and have nothing to do with Jerusalem. One explanation for their name is that they were christened gira-sole, "Jerusalem", because their yellow flowers turned towards the sun. The Italian name for the Jerusalem artichoke is *girasole articocco*.

These small knobbly tubers have a lovely distinct flavour and are good in Palestine soup, a popular classic recipe. They are also delicious baked or braised.

History

Jerusalem artichokes are thought to have come from the central United States and Canada, where they were cultivated by the American-Indians as long ago as the fifteenth century. However, many writers have alluded to the fact that they cause "wind", which tempers their popularity.

Buying and Storing

Jerusalem artichokes are at their best during winter and early spring. They are invariably knobbly but if possible buy neat ones with the minimum of knobs to save waste. The skins should be pale brown without any dark or soft patches. If they are stored in a cool dark place they will keep well for up to 10 days.

Preparing

The white flesh of artichokes turns pur-plish brown when exposed to light, so when peeling or slicing them raw, place them in a bowl of acidulated water (water to which the juice of about half a lemon has been added). Because artichokes are so knobbly, it is often easier to boil them in acidulated water in their skins and peel them afterwards – the cooked skins should slip off easily.

Cooking

Jerusalem artichokes can be cooked in many of the ways in which you would cook potatoes or parsnips. They are excellent roasted, sautéed or dipped in batter and fried, but first par-boil them for 10-15 minutes until nearly tender. For creamed artichokes, mix with potatoes in equal amounts; this slightly blunts their flavour, making a tasty side dish which is not too overpowering.

Left: Parsnips.
Below: Jerusalem artichokes.

TURNIPS AND SWEDES

Turnips and swedes are both members of the cabbage family and are closely related to each other – so close that it is not surprising that their names are often confused. For instance, swedes are sometimes called Swedish turnips or swede-turnips and in Scotland, where they are thought of as turnips, they are called neeps.

Nowadays, the confusion is not so acute. Many greengrocers and super-markets sell early or baby turnips or, better still, French turnips – *navets*.

Both are small and white, tinged either with green or in the case of *navets*, with pink or purple. Consequently, people are learning to tell their swedes from their turnips and also discovering what a deli-cious vegetable the turnip is.

History

Turnips have been cultivated for cen-turies, principally as an important live-stock feed but also for humans. Although they were not considered the food of gourmets, they have been grown by

poorer families as a useful addition to the winter table.

Swedes were known as turnip-rooted cabbages until the 1780s, when Sweden began exporting the vegetable to Britain and the shorter name resulted.

Until recently, turnips and swedes have not enjoyed a very high reputation among cooks in many parts of the world. This is partly because they are perceived as cattle food and partly because few people have taken the trouble to find acceptable ways of cooking them. Schools and other institutions tend to boil and then mash them to a watery pulp, and for many people this is the only way they have eaten either vegetable.

The French, in contrast, have had far more respect for the turnip, at least. For centuries they have devised recipes for their delicate *navets*, roasting them, caramelizing them in sugar and butter or simply steaming and serving with butter. Young, tender turnips have also been popular all over the Mediterranean region for many years, and there are many dishes using turnips with fish, poultry, or teamed with tomatoes, onions and spinach.

Nutrition

Both turnips and swedes are a good source of calcium and potassium.

Varieties

French *navets*, small round, squashed-shaped turnips tinged with pink or purple, are increasingly available in greengrocers and supermarkets in the spring. Less common, but even more prized by the French, are the long carrot-shaped turnips, called *vertus*. English turnips are generally larger and are mainly green and white.

Both have the characteristic peppery flavour, but this is less pronounced in *navets* which are generally sweeter.

Swedes generally have a more substantial, fuller-bodied flavour than turnips but at their best have a subtle, pleasant taste. The Marian is a yellow fleshed variety with a distinct "swede" flavour. White fleshed swedes, like Merrick, have a more watery, turnip-like flavour.

Buying and Storing

Turnips: If possible, buy French *navets* or failing that, the smallest and youngest turnips, available in the shops from spring. They should be firm, smooth and unblemished, ideally with fresh green tops. Store in a cool dry place.
Swedes: Unlike turnips, swedes generally seem to come large. However, if possible, choose small swedes with smooth and unblemished skins as large ones are likely to be tough and fibrous. Store as for turnips.

Preparing and Cooking

Turnips: Young turnips should not need peeling; simply trim, then simmer or steam until tender. They are delicious raw, thinly sliced or grated into salads.

Peel older turnips (*below*) and then slice or dice before cooking. Remember, turnips are members of the cabbage family and older specimens particularly can show signs of that unpleasant cabbage rankness if overcooked. To avoid this, blanch turnips if they are to be served as a vegetable dish, or add sparingly to soups and casseroles, so that the rank flavour is dispersed.

Swedes: Peel to remove the skin and then cut into chunks (*below*). Swedes will disintegrate if overcooked, and they are unpleasantly raw tasting if not cooked sufficiently. The only answer is to check frequently while they are cooking. Swedes are particularly good when teamed with other root vegetables in soups and casseroles, adding a pleasant, slightly nutty flavour.

*Far left: Navets and Turnips.
Below: Swedes.*

CARROTS

After potatoes, carrots are without doubt our best-known and best-loved root vegetable. In the days when vegetables were served merely as an accessory to meat, carrots always made an appearance – often overcooked but still eaten up because, we were told, they helped you to see in the dark.

Carrots have many different flavours, depending on how they are cooked. Young, new season carrots braised in butter and a splash of water are intensely flavoured and sweet; when steamed, they are tender and melting. Carrots grated into salads are fresh and clean tasting, while in casseroles they are savoury with the characteristic carrot flavour. In soups they are fragrant and mild, and in cakes their flavour can hardly be detected, yet their sweetness adds richness.

History

Until the Middle Ages, carrots were purple. The orange carrots came from Holland, from where they were exported in the seventeenth and eighteenth centuries. Although purple and white carrots continued to be eaten in France, nowadays they are something of a rarity.

Nutrition

Carrots contain large amounts of carotene and vitamin A, along with useful amounts of vitamins B3, C and E. When eaten raw, they also provide good quantities of potassium, calcium, iron and zinc, but these are reduced when carrots are boiled.

The idea that carrots are good for your night sight originated in the Second World War. Early radar stations were established along the south and east coasts of England in 1939 to detect aggressors in the air or at sea. The Germans attributed this sudden remarkable night vision to the British habit of eating carrots. Indeed, the vitamin A in carrots forms retinal, a lack of which brings on night blindness.

Buying and Storing

Home-grown carrots are so much nicer than shop bought ones. Almost all vegetables have a better flavour if grown organically, but this is particularly true of carrots.

When buying carrots, look out for the very young, pencil thin ones, which are beautifully tender either eaten raw or steamed for just a few minutes. Young carrots are commonly sold with their feathery tops intact, which should be fresh and green. Older carrots should be firm and unblemished. Avoid tired looking carrots as they will have little nutritional value.

Carrots should not be stored for too long. They will keep for several days if stored in a cool, airy place or in the salad drawer of the fridge.

Preparing

Preparation depends on the age of the carrots. The valuable nutrients lie either in or just beneath the skin, so if the carrots are young, simply wash them under cold running water. Medium-size carrots may need to be scraped and large carrots will need either scraping or peeling.

Cooking

Carrots are excellent cooked or raw. Children often like raw carrots as they have a very sweet flavour. They can be cut into julienne strips, with a dressing added, or grated into salads and coleslaw – their juices run and blend wonderfully with the dressing. Carrots can be cooked in almost any way you choose. As an accompaniment, cut them into julienne strips and braise in butter and cider, or cook in the minimum of stock and toss in butter and a sprinkling of caraway seeds.

Roasted carrots are delicious, with a melt-in-the-mouth sweetness. Par-boil large ones first, but younger carrots can be quickly blanched or added direct to the pan with a joint of meat.

HORSERADISH

Horseradish is grown for its pungent root, which is normally grated and mixed with cream or oil and vinegar and served with roast beef. Fresh horseradish is available in many supermarkets in the spring, and you can make your own horseradish sauce by simply peeling the root and then mixing 45ml/3 tbsp grated horseradish with 150ml/$\frac{1}{4}$ pint/$\frac{2}{3}$ cup whipping cream and adding a little Dijon mustard, vinegar and sugar to taste. As well as being excellent with hot or cold beef, horseradish sauce is delicious with smoked trout or mackerel or spread thinly on sandwiches with a fine pâté.

Left: Carrots.
Right: Horseradish.

BEETROOT

Experience of vinegar-sodden beetroot has doubtlessly put many people off beetroot. Those who love it know to buy their beetroot fresh, so that they can cook it themselves. It can be served in a number of different ways: baked and served with soured cream, braised in a creamy sauce, grated in a salad or used for the classic soup *borscht*.

History

Beetroot is closely related to sugar beet and mangelwurzels. As the demand for sugar increased over the centuries, when sugar could successfully be extracted from beet, sugar production became a big industry in Britain and Europe.

Mangelwurzels were eaten in parts of Europe and in England in times of famine, although they were primarily grown as cattle fodder.

Beetroot, however, has probably been eaten since Roman times. By the mid-nineteenth century it was clearly a popular vegetable, and Mrs Beeton in her famous cookbook has 11 recipes for it, including a beetroot and carrot jam and beetroot fritters.

Nutrition

Beetroot is an excellent provider of potassium. The leaves, which have the flavour of spinach, are high in vitamin A, iron and calcium.

Buying and Storing

If possible, buy small beetroots which have their whiskers intact and have at least 5cm/2in of stalk at the top; if they are too closely cropped they will bleed during cooking. Beetroots will keep for several weeks if stored in a cool place.

Preparing

To cook beetroot whole, first rinse under cold running water. Cut the stalks to about 2.5cm/1in above the beetroot and don't cut away the root or peel it – or the glorious deep red colour will bleed away. When serving cold in salads, or where the recipe calls for chopped or grated beetroot, peel away the skin with a potato peeler or sharp knife.

Cooking

To bake in the oven, place the cleaned beetroot in a dish with a tight-fitting lid, and add 60-75ml/4-5 tbsp of water. Lay a double layer of foil over the dish before covering with the lid, then bake in a low oven for 2-3 hours or until the beetroot is tender. Check occasionally to ensure the pan doesn't dry out and to see whether the beetroot is cooked. It is ready when the skin begins to wrinkle and can be easily rubbed away with your fingers. Alternatively, simply wrap the beetroot in a double layer of foil and cook as above. To boil beetroot, prepare as above and simmer for about 1½ hours.

BEET GREENS

The tops of several root vegetables are not only edible, but are also extremely nutritious. Beet greens are particularly good, being very high in vitamins A and C, and indeed have more iron and calcium than spinach itself. They are delicious, but not easily available unless you grow your own. If you are lucky enough to get some, boil the greens for a few minutes, then drain well and serve with butter or olive oil.

Left: Beetroot.
Above right: Scorzonera.
Below right: Salsify.

SALSIFY AND SCORZONERA

These two root vegetables are closely related to each other as well as to members of the same family as dandelion and lettuce. All have long tapering roots.

Salsify has a white or pale brownish skin and scorzonera, sometimes called black salsify, has a black skin. They both have a pale creamy flesh and a fairly similar flavour reminiscent of artichokes and asparagus. Salsify is said to have the superior flavour and has been likened to oysters (it is sometimes referred to as the oyster plant), although many people fail to detect this.

Both salsify and scorzonera make an unusual and pleasant accompaniment, either creamed or fried in butter. They can also be also used in soups.

History

Salsify is native to the Mediterranean but now grows in most areas of Europe and North America. Scorzonera is a southern European plant.

Both roots are classified as herbs and, like many wild plants and herbs, their history is bound up with their use in medicines. The roots, together with their leaves and flowers, were used for the treatment of heartburn, loss of appetite and various liver diseases.

Buying and Storing

Choose specimens that are firm and smooth and, if possible, still with their tops on, which should look fresh and lively. Salsify will keep for several days stored in a cool dark place.

Preparing

Salsify and scorzonera are difficult to clean and peel. Either scrub the root under cold running water and then peel after cooking, or peel with a sharp stainless steel knife (*below*). As the flesh discolours quickly, place the trimmed pieces into acidulated water (water to which lemon juice has been added).

Cooking

Cut into short lengths and simmer for 20–30 minutes until tender. Drain well and sauté in butter, or serve with lemon juice, melted butter or chopped parsley.

Alternatively, they can be puréed for soups or mashed. Cooked and cooled salsify and scorzonera can be served in a mustard or garlic vinaigrette with a simple salad.

EXOTIC ROOTS

Throughout the tropical regions of the world all sorts of tubers are grown and used for a fabulous variety of dishes. Yams, sweet potatoes, cassava and taro, to name but a few, are for many people a staple food, not only cooked whole as a vegetable accompaniment, but ground or pounded for bread and cakes. There is an enormous variety of these tropical and subtropical tubers, and while they cannot be cultivated in a moderate climate, the more common tubers are now widely available in specialist shops and in most supermarkets.

SWEET POTATOES

Sweet potatoes are another one of those vegetables that once tasted, are never forgotten. They are, as the name suggests, sweet, but they also have a slightly spicy taste. It's this distinct sweet and savoury flavour which makes them such an excellent foil to many savoury dishes

and they are fittingly paired with meat dishes that need a touch of sweetness, like turkey or pork.

History

Sweet potatoes are native to tropical America, but today they are grown all over the tropical world. They have been grown in South America from before the Inca civilizations and were introduced into Spain before the ordinary potato. They also have a long history of cultivation in Asia spreading from Polynesia to New Zealand in the fourteenth century.

They are an important staple food in the Caribbean and southern United States, and many famous recipes feature these vegetables. Candied sweet potatoes, for instance, are traditionally served with ham or turkey at Thanksgiving all over the United States, while Jamaica and the West Indies abound with sweet potato dishes, from the simple baked

potato to Caribbean pudding, a typically sweet and spicy dish with sweet potatoes, coconut, limes and cinnamon.

Sweet potatoes appear to have been introduced to England even earlier than regular potatoes. Henry VIII was said to have been very partial to them baked in a pie, believing they would improve his love life! If Henry VIII was eating sweet potatoes in the early/mid-sixteenth century, then it's likely he received them via the Spanish, who, thanks to Christopher Columbus, were busy conquering the New World, thus experiencing a whole range of tropical vegetables and fruit.

Varieties

The skin colour ranges from white to pink to reddish brown. The red-skinned variety, which has a whitish flesh, is the one most commonly used in African and Caribbean cooking.

Buying and Storing

Choose small or medium-size ones if possible as larger specimens tend to be rather fibrous. They should be firm and evenly shaped; avoid those that seem withered, have damp patches or are sprouting. They will keep for several days in a cool place.

Preparing and Cooking

If baking, scrub the potatoes well and cook exactly as you would for ordinary potatoes. To boil, either cook in their skins and remove these after cooking, or peel and place in acidulated water (water to which lemon juice has been added). This prevents them turning brown and it's worth boiling them in lightly acidulated water for the same reason. Sweet potatoes can be cooked in any of the ways you would cook ordinary potatoes - roast, boiled, mashed or baked. However, avoid using them in creamy or gratin-type dishes. They are both too sweet and too spicy for that.

It is preferable to roast or sauté them with onions and other savoury ingredients to bring out their flavour, or mash them and serve them American-style over chunks of chicken for a crusted chicken pie.

YAMS

Yams have been a staple food for many cultures for thousands of years. There are today almost countless varieties, of different shapes, sizes and colours and called different names by different people. Most varieties are thought to have been native to China, although they found their way to Africa at a very early period and became a basic food, being easy to grow in tropical and subtropical conditions, and containing the essential carbohydrate of all staple foods.

Although cush-cush or Indian yam was indigenous to America, most yams were introduced to the New World as a result of the slave trade in the sixteenth century. Today with such a huge variety of this popular vegetable available, there are innumerable recipes for yam, many probably not printed and published, but handed down by word of mouth from mother to daughter and making their appearance at mealtimes all over the hot regions of the world.

Varieties

The greater yam, as the name suggests, can grow to a huge size. A weight of 62kg/150lb has been recorded. The varieties you are likely to find in shops will be about the size of a small marrow, although smaller yams are also available such as the sweet yam, which looks like a large potato and is normally covered with whiskery roots. All sizes have a coarse brown skin and can be white or red-fleshed.

In Chinese stores, you may find the Chinese yam, which is a more elongated, club-like shape and is covered with fine whiskers.

Buying

Look out for firm specimens with unbroken skins. The flesh inside should be creamy and moist and if you buy from a grocery, the shopkeeper may well cut open a yam so you can check that it is fresh. They can be stored for several weeks in a cool, dark place.

Preparing

Peel away the skin thickly to remove the outer skin and the layer underneath that contains the poison dioscorine. This in fact is destroyed during cooking, but discard the peel carefully. Place the peeled yam in salted water as it discolours easily.

Cooking

Yams, like potatoes, are used as the main starchy element in a meal, boiled and mashed, fried, sautéed or roasted. They tend to have an affinity with spicy sauces and are delicious cut into discs, fried and sprinkled with a little salt and cayenne pepper. African cooks frequently pound boiled yam to make a dough which is then served with spicy stews and soups.

TARO/EDDO

Like yams, taro is another hugely important tuber in tropical areas, and for thousands of years it has been a staple food for many people. It goes under many different names; in South-east Asia, South and Central America, all over Africa and in the Caribbean it is called variously eddo and dasheen.

There are two basic varieties of taro - a large barrel-shaped tuber and a smaller variety, which is often called eddo or dasheen. They are all a dark mahogany brown with a rather shaggy skin, looking like a cross between a beetroot and a swede.

Although they look very similar, taro belongs to a completely different family from yam and in flavour and texture is noticeably different. Boiled, it has a completely unique flavour, something like a floury water chestnut.

Buying and Storing

Try to buy small specimens; the really small smooth bulbs are tiny attachments to the larger taro and are either called eddoes, or rather sweetly, "sons of taro". Stored in a cool, dark place, they should keep for several weeks.

Left: Sweet potatoes.
Above: Yams.

Preparing

Taros, like yams, contain a poison just under the skin which produces an allergic reaction. Consequently, either peel taros thickly, wearing rubber gloves, or cook in their skins. The toxins are completely eliminated by boiling, and the skins peel off easily.

Cooking

Taros soak up large quantities of liquid during cooking, and this can be turned to advantage by cooking in well flavoured stock or with tomatoes and other vegetables. For this reason, they are excellent in soups and casseroles, adding bulk and flavour in a similar way to potatoes. They can also be steamed or boiled, deep-fried or puréed for fritters but must be served hot as they become sticky if allowed to cool.

CALLALOO

Callaloo are the leaves of the taro plant, poisonous if eaten raw, but used widely in Asian and Caribbean recipes. They are cooked thoroughly, then used for wrapping meat and vegetables. Callaloo can also be shredded and cooked together with pork, bacon, crab, prawns, okra, chilli, onions and garlic, together with lime and coconut milk to make one of the Caribbean's most famous dishes, named after the leaves themselves, Callaloo.

JICAMA

Also known as the Mexican potato, this large root vegetable is a native of central America. It has a thin brown skin and white, crunchy flesh which has a sweet, nutty taste. It can be eaten cooked in the same way as potatoes or sliced and added raw to salads.

Buy specimens that are firm to the touch. Jicama in good condition will keep for about two weeks if stored in a plastic bag in the refrigerator.

Top: Taros (Eddoes).
Above: Jicama.
Left: Callaloo.

CASSAVA

This is another very popular West Indian root, used in numerous Caribbean dishes. It is native to Brazil, and found its way to the West Indies surprisingly via Africa, where it also became a popular vegetable. Known as cassava in the West Indies, it is called manioc or mandioc in Brazil, and juca or yucca is used in other parts of South America.

Cassava is used to make tapioca, and in South America a sauce and an intoxicating beverage are prepared from the juice. However, in Africa and the West Indies it is eaten as a vegetable either boiled, baked or fried, or cooked and pounded to a dough to make *fufu*, a traditional savoury African pudding.

Right: Cassava.
Below left: Ginger.
Below right: Galangal.

GINGER AND GALANGAL

GINGER

This is probably the world's most important and popular spice and is associated with a number of different cuisines - Chinese, Indian and Caribbean, to name but a few. It was known in Europe during the Roman period, but was still fairly rare until the spice routes opened up trade in the sixteenth and seventeenth centuries. Like many spices, ginger has the quality of enhancing and complementing both sweet and savoury food, adding a fragrant spiciness to all sorts of dishes. However, while ground ginger is best in recipes which will be baked, and stem ginger, where the ginger is preserved in syrup, tastes wonderful in desserts, for savoury dishes, always use fresh root ginger.

Nowadays, the pale, knobbly roots of fresh ginger are widely available in supermarkets and whenever possible, buy just a small quantity, as you will not need a great deal and fresh ginger will not keep indefinitely.

To prepare, simply peel away the skin with a sharp knife and grate or thinly slice according to the recipe.

GREATER GALANGAL

Galangal looks similar to ginger except that the rhizome is thinner and the young shoots are bright pink. The roots should be prepared in the same way as ginger and can be used in curries and satay sauces.

FOUR

GREENS

Spinach

Brussels Sprouts

Cauliflower

Sprouting Broccoli
and Calabrese

Turnip Tops

Cabbage

Kale and Curly Kale

Garden and Wild Leaves

Chinese Greens

Kohlrabi

Swiss Chard

SPINACH

For many people, spinach is inextricably linked with Popeye, the cartoon character who used to eat huge amounts of spinach. It is a wonderfully versatile vegetable, popular worldwide, with nearly every cuisine featuring spinach somewhere in its repertoire. The Italians are particularly partial to spinach and have hundreds of dishes using the vegetable. The words *à la florentine* mean the dish contains spinach.

As well as being delicious on its own, chopped or puréed spinach can be mixed with a range of other ingredients with superb results. It has a particular affinity with dairy products and in the Middle East, feta or helim cheese is used to make boreks or other spinach pies. The Italians mix spinach with ricotta or Parmesan cheese for a huge range of recipes, and the English use eggs and sometimes Cheddar for a spinach soufflé.

History

Spinach was first cultivated in Persia several thousands of years ago. It came to Europe via the Arab world; the Moors introduced it to Spain, and Arabs in the Middle East took it to Greece. It first appeared in England in the fourteenth century, probably via Spain. It is mentioned in the first known English cookery book, where it is referred to as *spynoches*; which echoes the Spanish word for spinach which is *espinacas*. It quickly became a popular vegetable, probably because it is quick and easy to grow and similarly easy and quick to cook.

Nutrition

Spinach is an excellent source of vitamin C if eaten raw, as well as vitamins A and B, calcium, potassium and iron. Spinach was originally thought to provide far more iron than it actually does, but the iron is "bound" up by oxalic acid in cooked spinach, which prevents the body absorbing anything but the smallest amounts. Even so, it is still an extremely healthy vegetable whether eaten cooked or raw.

Buying and Storing

Spinach grows all year round, so you should have no difficulty in buying it fresh. Frozen spinach is a poor substitute, mainly because it has so little flavour, so it is worth the effort to use the fresh product.

Spinach leaves should be green and lively; if they look tired and the stalks are floppy, shop round until you find something in better condition. Spinach reduces significantly when cooked; about 450g/1lb will serve two people. Store it in the salad drawer of the fridge, where it will keep for 1-2 days.

Preparing

Wash well in a bowl of cold water and remove any tough or large stalks.

Cooking

Throw the leaves into a large pan with just the water that clings to the leaves and place over a low heat with a sprinkling of salt. Cover the pan so the spinach steams in its own liquid and shake the pan occasionally to prevent the spinach sticking to the bottom. It cooks in 4-6 minutes, wilting down to about an eighth of its former volume. Drain and press out the remaining liquid with the back of a spoon.

Spinach can be used in a variety of ways. It can be chopped and served with lots of butter, or similarly served with other spring vegetables such as

BRUSSELS SPROUTS

baby carrots or young broad beans. For frittatas, chop the spinach finely, stir in a little Parmesan cheese, a good sprinkling of salt and pepper and a dash of cream, if liked, and stir into the omelette before cooking. Alternatively, purée it for sauces or blend it for soups. Spinach is also delicious raw, served with chopped bacon or croûtons. A fresh spinach salad is delicious as the leaves have just the right balance of flavour – sharp but not overpowering.

Below: Spinach.
Below right: Brussels sprouts.

Brussels sprouts have a pronounced and sweet nutty flavour, quite unlike cabbage, although the two are closely related. They are traditionally served at Christmas with chestnuts and indeed have a definite affinity for certain nuts – particularly the sweet flavoured nuts, e.g. almonds pair well rather than hazelnuts or walnuts.

History

Brussels sprouts were cultivated in Flanders (now Belgium) during the Middle Ages. They are basically miniature cabbages which grow in a knobbly row on a long tough stalk. The Germans call sprouts *rosenkohl* – rose cabbage – a pretty and descriptive name as they look like small rosebuds.

Buying and Storing

Buy Brussels sprouts as fresh as possible as older ones are more likely to have that strong unpleasant "cabbage" flavour. They should be small and hard with tightly wrapped leaves. Avoid any

that are turning yellow or brown or have loose leaves.

Brussels sprouts will keep for several days in a cool place such as a larder or salad drawer of a fridge, but it is far better to buy them as you need them.

Preparing

Cut away the bottom of the stalk and remove the outer leaves. Some people cut a cross through the bottom of the stalk although this is not really necessary. If you haven't been able to avoid buying big Brussels sprouts, cut them in half or into quarters, or slice them thinly for stir-frying.

Cooking

As with cabbage, either cook Brussels sprouts very briefly or braise slowly in the oven. Cook in small amounts of fast boiling water for about 3 minutes until just tender. To stir-fry Brussel sprouts, slice into three or four pieces and then fry in a little oil and butter – they taste great with onions and ginger.

CAULIFLOWER

Cauliflower is a member of the cabbage family, *Brassica oleracea*. Like all cabbages, cauliflower suffers terribly from overcooking. A properly cooked cauliflower has a pleasant fresh flavour but when overcooked it turns grey and becomes unpalatably soft, taking on a nasty rank flavour with an unpleasant aftertaste. Children often like raw cauliflower even though they may not connect it with the same vegetable served up at school.

History

Cauliflower is thought to have come originally from China and thence to the Middle East. The Moors introduced it to Spain in the twelfth century and from there it found its way to England via established trading routes. The early cauliflower was the size of a tennis ball but they have gradually been cultivated to the enormous sizes we see today. Ironically, baby cauliflowers are now fashionable.

Varieties

Green and occasionally purple cauliflowers are available in the shops. The purple variety was originally grown in Sardinia and Italy but is increasingly grown by other market gardeners. They look pretty and unusual but are otherwise similar to white cauliflowers.

Dwarf varieties of cauliflowers are now commonly available in shops, as well as baby white cauliflowers.

Romanescoes: These pretty green or white vegetables look like a cross between broccoli and cauliflower, but are more closely related to cauliflowers. They taste very much like cauliflowers, but since they are quite small, they are less likely to be overcooked and consequently retain their excellent flavour.

Broccoflower: A cross between broccoli and cauliflower, this looks like a pale green cauliflower. It has a mild flavour and should be cooked in the same way as you would cauliflower.

Right: Baby cauliflowers.
Far right top: Romanescoes.
Far right bottom: Green cauliflowers.

Nutrition

Cauliflower contains potassium, iron and zinc, although cooking reduces the amounts. It is also a good source of vitamins A and C.

Buying and Storing

In top condition, a cauliflower is a creamy white colour with the outer leaves curled round the flower. The head should be unblemished with no black or discoloured areas and the outer leaves should look fresh and crisp. Keep cauliflower in a cool place for no longer than 1-2 days; after that it will deteriorate and valuable nutrients will be lost.

Preparing

To cook a cauliflower whole, first trim away the coarse bottom leaves (leave the inner ones on, if liked). Very large cauliflowers are best halved or broken into florets, as the outside will overcook before the inside is tender. Some people trim away the stalk, but others like this part and only trim off the very thick stalk at the bottom of the plant.

Cooking

Cauliflowers are excellent steamed, either whole or in florets. Place in a steamer or colander over a pan of boiling water, cover and steam until just tender and immediately remove from the heat. The florets can then be fried in olive oil or butter for a few minutes to give a lightly browned finish.

When cooking a cauliflower whole, start testing it after 10 minutes; it should feel tender but still have plenty of "bite" left in it. Cauliflower is a popular vegetable accompaniment, either served with just a little butter, or with a tomato or cheese sauce. It is also good stir-fried with onions and garlic together with a few tomatoes and capers.

Cauliflower is excellent in salads or used for crudités. Either use it raw or blanch it in boiling water for 1-2 minutes, then refresh under cold running water.

Small cauliflowers and romanescoes are intended to be cooked whole, and can be steamed or boiled, covered with a lid, in the minimum of water for 4-5 minutes until just tender.

SPROUTING BROCCOLI <u>AND</u> CALABRESE

Varieties

Calabrese Broccoli: This is the vegetable we today commonly call broccoli, with large beautiful, blue-green heads on succulent stalks. It is named after the Italian province of Calabria where this variety was first developed.

Purple Sprouting Broccoli: The original variety – has long thin stalks with small flowerheads that are normally purple but can be white or green. Heads, stalks and tender leaves are all edible. The purple heads turn green when cooked but the others keep their colour. Purple sprouting broccoli is more seasonal than the easily available calabrese; it is usually available from late winter onwards.

Buying and Storing

If possible, buy loose broccoli rather than the pre-wrapped bundles, because it is easier to check that it is fresh and also because wrapped vegetables tend to deteriorate more quickly.

Purple sprouting broccoli can also be sold loose or prepacked. Check that the stalk, flowerhead and leaves all look fresh and that the flowerlets are tightly closed and bright green. Neither type will keep for long.

Broccoli or calabrese is a relatively modern vegetable and is one of the most popular. It is quick and easy to prepare with little or no waste and similarly easy to cook. It is attractive, whether served raw or cooked, and you can buy it in the quantity you require, unlike cauliflower or cabbage.

History

Before calabrese came into our shops, people bought and ate purple sprouting broccoli. This is basically an "untidy" version of calabrese, with long shoots and clusters of flowerheads at the end – the broccoli we know today has neat tidy heads. The stalks of purple sprouting broccoli have a faint asparagus flavour.

The Romans cooked purple sprouting broccoli in wine or served it with sauces and it is still a popular vegetable today in Italy, cooked in the oven with anchovies and onions or served with pasta in a garlic and tomato sauce.

Preparing and Cooking

Trim the ends and remove any discoloured leaves.

Calabrese Broccoli: Break into even-size pieces, dividing the stem and flowerhead lengthways if they are thick. Cook in a little boiling water for 4-5 minutes until just tender and then drain. Do not steam this variety of broccoli as its vibrant green colour tends to turn grey.

Purple Sprouting Broccoli: Either steam in long, even-size lengths in a steamer or, if you have an asparagus kettle, cook as you would asparagus. Alternatively, tie the stems loosely together and stand in a little water – if necessary, wedge it in with a potato or rolled up piece of foil. Cover with a dome of foil and steam for 4-5 minutes until tender.

Serving

Serve both varieties simply with butter and lemon juice or with a Hollandaise or Béarnaise sauce as an accompaniment. They are also excellent stir-fried.

Above far left: Purple cauliflower.
Below far left: Purple sprouting broccoli.
Above: Calabrese broccoli.

TURNIP TOPS

Turnip tops, like beet greens, are both delicious and nutritious. They are not widely available but if you are able to buy some or if you grow your own, slice them *(below)* and boil or steam for a few minutes, then drain and serve with butter.

CABBAGE

Cabbage, sliced and cooked, can be one of two things: deliciously crisp, with a mild pleasant flavour – or overcooked and horrible! Cabbage and other brassicas contain the chemical hydrogen sulphide, which is activated during cooking at about the point the vegetable starts to soften. It eventually disappears, but during the in-between time, cabbage acquires its characteristic rank smell and flavour. So, either cook cabbage briefly, or cook it long and slow, preferably with other ingredients so that flavours can mingle.

History

Cabbage has a long and varied history. However, because there are many varieties of cabbage under the general heading of "brassica", it is difficult to be sure whether the variety the Greeks and Romans enjoyed is the same as today's round cabbage, or something more akin to kale or even Chinese cabbage.

The round cabbages we know today were an important food during the Dark Ages, and by the Middle Ages they were in abundance, as you will see if you study the paintings of that period. These commonly show kitchen tables or baskets at market positively groaning with fruit and vegetables, and cabbages in all their shapes and sizes were often featured.

Medieval recipes suggest cooking cabbages with leeks, onions and herbs. In the days when all except the very wealthy cooked everything in one pot, it is fair to assume that cabbages were cooked long and slow until fairly recently.

Varieties

Savoy Cabbage: This is a variety of green cabbage with crimped or curly leaves. It has a mild flavour and is particularly tender, thus needing less cooking than other varieties.

Spring Greens: These have fresh loose heads with a pale yellow-green heart. They are available in spring and are delicious simply sliced, steamed and served with butter.

Right: Savoy cabbage.
Above far right: Green cabbage.
Below far right: Spring greens.

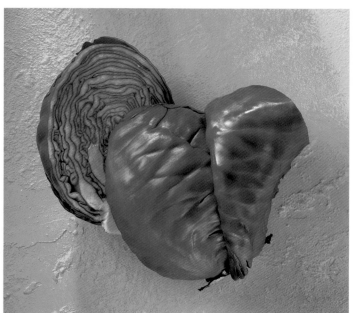

Green Cabbage: The early green, or spring, cabbages are dark green, loose leafed and have a slightly pointed head. They have little or no heart as they are picked before this has had time to develop. Nevertheless, they are a very good cabbage and all but the very outside leaves should be tender. As the season progresses, larger, firmer and more pale green cabbages are available. These are a little tougher than the spring cabbages and need longer cooking.

Red Cabbage: A beautifully coloured cabbage with smooth firm leaves. The colour fades during cooking unless a little vinegar is added to the water. Red cabbage can be pickled or stewed with spices and flavourings.

White Cabbage: Sometimes called Dutch cabbages, white cabbages have smooth firm pale green leaves. They are available throughout the winter. They are good cooked or raw. To cook, slice them thinly, then boil or steam and serve with butter. To serve raw, slice thinly and use in a coleslaw.

Buying and Storing

Cabbages should be fresh looking and unblemished. When buying, avoid any with wilted leaves or those that look or feel puffy. Savoys and spring greens will keep in a cool place for several days; firmer cabbages will keep happily for much longer.

Preparing

Remove the outer leaves, if necessary, and then cut into quarters. Remove the stalk and then slice or shred according to your recipe or to taste.

Cooking

For green or white cabbages, place the shredded leaves in a pan with a knob of butter and a couple of tablespoons of water to prevent burning. Cover and cook over a medium heat until the leaves are tender, occasionally shaking the pan or stirring.

Red cabbage is cooked quite differently and is commonly sautéed in oil or butter and then braised in a low oven for up to $1\frac{1}{2}$ hours with apples, currants, onions, vinegar, wine, sugar and spices.

KALE AND CURLY KALE

Kale is the name used for a variety of green leafed vegetable of the brassica family. Most kales have thick stems and robust leaves that do not form a head. Many kales have curly leaves, which are the variety most commonly eaten. Large coarse-leafed kales are grown for cattle and sheep feeds.

History

Kale is thought to be one of the first culti-vated brassicas. Colewort, the wild ancestor, still grows along the coasts of western Europe.

Varieties

Collards: Collards, or collard greens, are a popular green vegetable in the south-ern United States. They are grown in summer and autumn for harvesting in the spring and are a good source of vitamin A.
Curly Kale: With its crimped, curly leaves, this is the most commonly avail-able kale, although even this can be quite hard to come by. If you are a big fan and don't grow your own, try farm shops in early spring.
Purple or Silver Kale: This is an orna-mental variety, and is grown almost exclusively for display.

Preparing and Cooking

Kale is probably the strongest tasting of the brassicas and is best cooked simply, paired with a bland-flavoured vegetable, such as potatoes. To prepare, break the leaves from the stalk and then cut out any thick stalk from the leaf. This can then be rolled and sliced or cooked whole. Boil the leaves in a little salted water for 3-5 minutes until tender. Owing to its robust nature, kale is fre-quently teamed with fairly hot spices and is consequently popular in many Indian dishes.

Above far left: White cabbage.
Below far left: Red cabbage.
Left: Collards.
Above: Curly kale.

GARDEN AND WILD LEAVES

VINE LEAVES

All leaves from vines that produce grapes can be eaten when young. They make an ideal wrapping for various meats and vegetables as they are surprisingly strong and of course edible. Most countries that produce wine will have dishes where vine leaves appear. *Dolmades*, commonly eaten in Greece and the Middle East is perhaps the best known dish, but in France, Spain and Italy, there are recipes using vine leaves to wrap small birds, like quail or snipe.

Vine leaves have a faintly lemon/cabbage flavour which can be detected at its best in a good *dolmades*. The leaves need to be cooked briefly before using, so that they are pliable and don't crack or break as you wrap the food. Bring to the boil and simmer for about 1 minute. The leaves should then be drained and separated until you are ready to use them.

DANDELION

Any child who has picked dandelions for his or her rabbits or guinea pigs and has watched them gobble them up greedily will know that this weed, though hated by the gardener in the family, has something going for it. Some gardeners, of course, are very partial to dandelion and raise the plant carefully so that the leaves are fresh and tender for the salad, and in France dandelions can often be seen for sale at market.

Look in any book of herbal remedies,

and dandelions will feature prominently. They are a well-known diuretic, their French name - *pissenlits* (piss-a-bed) – attesting to this in no uncertain terms.

Although it's gratifying to pick your own vegetables for free, it is generally recommended, if you like dandelions, that you buy the domestic seeds and grow your own. These are likely to be the juiciest

and least bitter plants. If you do pick your own, do so well away from the roadside and wash the leaves carefully.

Dandelion leaves can be added to salads or used in *pissenlits au lard*, where whole young dandelion plants are dressed in vinaigrette and then covered in finely chopped pieces of salt pork or bacon and bacon fat.

SORREL

Sorrel is not always available commercially, although it is in France and is greatly prized. However, it grows wild in cool soils or you could grow it in your own garden. Young leaves are delicious in salads, or, later in the year, use it in soups or sauces to accompany fish. It has a sharp, distinct, lemon flavour and is commonly teamed with eggs and cream.

ORACHE

Although not related to spinach, this beautiful red or golden-leaved plant is called mountain spinach and its large leaves can be treated like spinach.

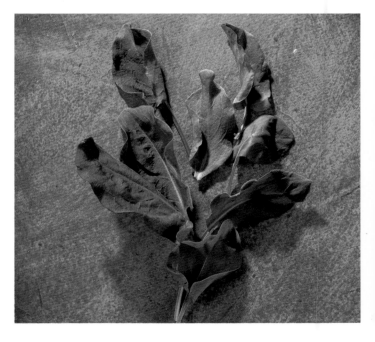

GOOD KING HENRY AND FAT HEN

These are both members of the goose-foot family and were popular vegetables in Tudor times. Today, Good King Henry has all but disappeared, and Fat Hen only grows wild as a weed. Both were superseded by spinach, which they are said to resemble in taste, although Fat Hen is milder.

NETTLES

Wild food enthusiasts get very excited about nettles as food, perhaps because they are plentiful and free and maybe because they take pleasure in eating something that everyone else avoids. Of course, once cooked, the sting completely disappears. They should be picked when they are very young and are good used in soups.

Above far left: Fresh vine leaves.
Above left: Dandelion.
Below left: Sorrel.
Right: Good King Henry.
Below: Nettles.

CHINESE GREENS

CHINESE CABBAGE/LEAVES (PE-TSAI)

Chinese cabbage, also called Napa cabbage, has pale green, crinkly leaves with long, wide, white ribs. Its shape is a little like a very fat head of celery, which gives rise to another of its alternative names, celery cabbage. It is pleasantly crunchy with a faint cabbage flavour and since it is available all year round, it makes a useful winter salad component. Chinese cabbage is also very good stir-fried with a tasty sauce. It is an essential ingredient of many oriental recipes.

Buying and Storing

For some reason, Chinese leaves almost always look fresh and perky when on sale in the supermarket, which probably indicates that they travel well and are transported quickly. Avoid any with discoloured or damaged stems. The leaves should be pale green and straight without blemishes or bruises. They will keep for up to six days in the salad drawer of the fridge.

Preparing

Remove the outside leaves and slice as much as you need.

Many Chinese greens are members of the brassica family. If you go into a popular and reasonably large Chinese supermarket, you'll be astonished at the varieties of green vegetables for sale. Discovering the name of these vegetables, on the other hand, can be a bit of a hit-and-miss undertaking, as the shop keepers, although always well intentioned, rarely know the English name, if indeed there is one.

CHINESE MUSTARD GREENS

Mustard greens are worth buying if you can, as they are very good to eat. The plant is a member of the cabbage family, but is grown in Europe solely for its mustard seed. In India and Asia it has long been grown for its oil seed, but the Chinese developed the plant for its leaves as well. These are deep green and slightly puckered-looking and have a definite mustard flavour, which can be quite fiery.

If you grow your own, then you'll be able to enjoy the young leaves which can be added to lettuce to spice up salads. Older leaves are best stir-fried and then dressed with a light Chinese sauce. They are also good cooked with onion and garlic and served as a side dish to accompany pork or bacon.

Preparing and Cooking

Break apart the stalks, rinse, then cut both stalks and leaves into thick or thin slices. These can then be stir-fried with garlic and onions, or cooked and served as you would Swiss chard. It has a pleasant flavour, milder than mustard greens, yet with more bite than the bland Chinese cabbage.

CHINESE BROCCOLI

This is another leafy vegetable, but with slender heads of flowers that look a little like our own broccoli, except that the flowers are usually white or yellow. Once the thicker stalks are trimmed, the greens can be sliced and cooked and served in the same way as Chinese mustard greens.

Far left: Chinese mustard greens.
Left: Chinese leaves.
Above: Chinese broccoli.
Below: Pak-Choi.

Cooking and Serving

If adding to salads, combine Chinese cabbage with something fairly forceful, like endive or rocket, and add a well-flavoured dressing. If adding to a stir-fry, cook with garlic, ginger and other fairly strong flavours. While the faint cabbage flavour will be lost, you will still get the pleasant crunchy "bite" of the stalk, and the leaves will carry the sauce.

PAK-CHOI

If you frequent your local Chinese super-market, you will almost certainly have come across *Pak-Choi*. In English it should correctly be called Chinese celery cabbage and its thick stalks, joined at the end in a small root, are vaguely celery-like. Its leaves, on the other hand, are generally large and spoon shaped. There are many different species of this vegetable, and smaller specimens look more like the tops of radish and have small slim stalks. Consequently the vegetable can be known by all sorts of picturesque names, like "horse's ear" and "horse's tail". There is no rule for discovering exactly what you are buying, but the important thing is to choose a fresh plant whatever its size: look for fresh green leaves and crisp stalks.

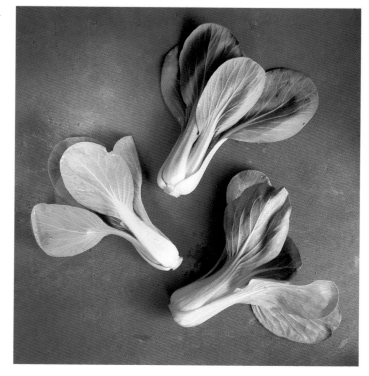

KOHLRABI

Kohlrabi looks like a cross between a cabbage and a turnip and is often classified as a root vegetable, even though it grows above ground. It is a member of the brassica family, but, unlike cabbages, it is the bulbous stalk that is edible rather than the flowering heads.

There are two varieties of kohlrabi: one is purple and the other pale green. They both have the same mild and fresh tasting flavour, not dissimilar to water chestnuts. It is neither as peppery as turnip nor as distinctive as cabbage, but it is easy to see why people think it a little like both. It can be served as an alternative to carrots or turnips.

History

Although kohlrabi is not a very popular vegetable in Britain, it is commonly eaten in other parts of Europe, as well as in China, India and Asia. In Kashmir, where it is grown extensively, there are many recipes – the bulbs are often finely sliced and eaten in salads and the greens are cooked in mustard oil with garlic and chillies.

Buying and Storing

Kohlrabi is best when small and young, since larger specimens tend to be coarse and fibrous. It keeps well for 7-10 days if stored in a cool place.

Preparing

Peel the skin with a knife and then cook whole or slice.

Cooking

Very small kohlrabi are tender and can be cooked whole. However, if they are any bigger than 5cm/2in in diameter, they can be stuffed. To do this, hollow out a little before cooking and then stuff with fried onions and tomatoes for instance. For sliced kohlrabi, cook until just tender and serve with butter or a creamy sauce. They can also be cooked long and slow in gratin dishes, with, for instance, potatoes as a variation of *Gratin Dauphinois*. Alternatively, par-boil them and bake in the oven covered with a cheese sauce.

SWISS CHARD

Swiss chard is one of those vegetables that needs plenty of water when growing, which explains why it is a popular garden vegetable in many places which have a high rainfall. Gardeners are very fond of Swiss chard, not only because it is delicious to eat but also because it is so very striking.

Swiss chard is often likened to spinach. The leaves have similarities, although they are not related and chard is on an altogether larger scale. Swiss chard leaves are large and fleshy with distinctive white ribs, and the flavour is stronger and more robust than spinach. It is popular in France where it is baked with rice, eggs and milk in *tians*, and cooked in a celebrated pastry from Nice – *tourte de blettes* – which is a sweet tart filled with raisins, pinenuts, apples and Swiss chard bound together with eggs. It is also often combined with eggs in frittatas and tortillas.

Swiss chard is a member of the beet family and is called by several names on this theme, including seakale beet and spinach beet.

Ruby or rhubarb chard has striking red ribs and leaf beet is often cultivated as a decorative plant, but they both have the same flavour, and unlike sugar beet and beetroot, they are cultivated only for their leaves.

Buying and Storing

Heads of chard should be fresh and bright green; avoid those with withered leaves or flabby stems. It keeps better than spinach but should be eaten within a couple of days.

Preparing

Some people buy or grow chard for the white stems alone and discard the leaves (or give them to pet guinea pigs), but this is a waste of a delicious vegetable. The leaf needs to be separated from the ribs, and this can be done roughly with a sharp knife (*right*) or more precisely using scissors. The ribs can then be sliced. Either shred the leaves, or blanch them and use them to wrap little parcels of fragrant rice or other food. If the chard is young and small, the ribs do not need to be removed.

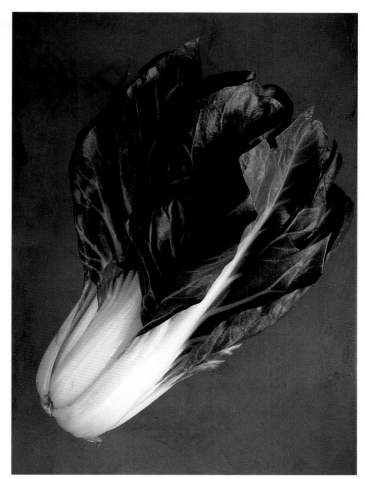

Cooking

For pies, frittatas and gratins, the leaves and ribs can be cooked together. Gently sauté the ribs in butter and oil and then add the leaves a minute or so later. Alternatively, the ribs can be simmered in a little water until tender and the leaves added a few minutes later or steamed over the top.

Above far left: Kohlrabi.
Left: Purple kohlrabi.
Above: Swiss chard.

BEANS, PEAS AND SEEDS

BROAD BEANS

One of the delights of having a garden is discovering how truly delicious some vegetables are when garden fresh. This seems particularly true of broad beans, which have a superb sweet flavour that sadly can never be reproduced in the frozen product. If you're lucky enough to grow or be given fresh broad beans, don't worry about recipes; just cook them until tender and serve with butter. It will be a revelation! However, if you're not one of those lucky few, don't dismiss broad beans, as they are still a wonderfully versatile vegetable. They can be used in soups or casseroles, and, since they have a mealy texture, they also purée well.

History

People have been eating broad beans almost since time began. A variety of wild broad bean grew all over southern Europe, North Africa and Asia, and they would have been a useful food for early man. There is archaeological evidence that by Neolithic times broad beans were being farmed, making them one of the first foods to be cultivated.

Broad beans will grow in most climates and most soils. They were a staple food for people throughout the Dark Ages and the Middle Ages, grown for feeding people and livestock until being replaced by the potato in the seventeenth and eighteenth centuries. Broad beans were an important source of protein for the poor, and because they dry well, they would have provided nourishing meals for families until the next growing season.

Nutrition

Beans are high in protein and carbohydrates and are also a good source of vitamins A, B1 and B2. They also provide potassium and iron as well as several other minerals.

Buying and Storing

Buy beans as fresh as possible. The pods should preferably be small and tender. Use as soon as possible.

Preparing

Very young beans in tender pods, no more than 7.5cm/3in in length, can be

eaten pod and all; top and tail, and then slice roughly. Usually, however, you will need to shell the beans. Elderly beans are often better skinned after they are cooked to rid them of the strong, bitter flavour that puts many people off this vegetable.

Cooking

Plunge shelled beans (or in their pods if very young) into rapidly boiling water and cook until just tender. They can also be par-boiled and then finished off braised in butter. For a simple broad bean purée, blend the cooked beans with garlic cooked in butter, cream and a pinch of fresh herbs, such as savory or thyme.

LIMA BEANS

These are popular in the US, named after the capital of Peru, and are sold mainly shelled. They are an essential ingredient in the American-Indian dish *succotash*. Lima beans should be cooked in a little boiling water until tender. Elderly beans need skinning after they are cooked. The dried bean, also known as the butter bean, can be large or small. These large beans tend to become mushy when cooked so are best used in soups or purées.

Above: Broad beans.
Below: Lima beans.
Right: Runner beans.

RUNNER BEANS

The runner bean is native to South America, where it has been cultivated for more than 2000 years and there is archaeological evidence of its existence much earlier than that.

It is a popular vegetable to grow. Most home vegetable gardeners have a patch of runner beans – they are easy to grow and, like all legumes, their roots contain bacteria that help renew nitrogen supplies in the soil.

They have a more robust flavour and texture than French beans and are distinct from green beans in several ways: they are generally much larger with long, flattened pods; their skin is rough textured, although in young beans this softens during cooking; and they contain purple beans within the pods, unlike green beans whose beans are mostly white or pale green. Nevertheless, runner beans belong to the same family as all the green beans.

Buying and Storing

Always buy young beans as the pods of larger beans are likely to be tough. The pods should feel firm and fresh; if you can see the outline of the bean inside the pod it is likely to be fibrous – although you could leave the beans to dry out and use the dried beans later in the season. Ideally, the beans inside should be no larger than your small fingernail.

Use as soon as possible after buying; they do not store well.

Preparing

Runner beans need to be topped and tailed and may also need stringing. Carefully put your knife through the top of the bean without cutting right through, and then pull downwards; if a thick thread comes away, the beans need stringing, so do the same on the other side. The beans can then be sliced either using a sharp knife or a slicer.

Slice through lengthways, not diagonally, so that you will be able to serve the beans with just a little skin and lots of succulent flesh.

Cooking

Plunge the beans into boiling salted water and cook until *al dente*.

PEAS

Fresh peas are wonderful – try tasting them raw, straight from the pod. Unfortunately, the season for garden peas is short, and frozen peas, which are the next best thing, never quite come up to the mark. If you grow your own peas, for three or four weeks in early summer, you can eat like kings; otherwise you can buy them from a good greengrocer, who may be able to keep you supplied all through the early summer.

History

Peas have an even longer history than broad beans, with archaeological evidence showing they were cultivated as long ago as 5700 BC. High in protein and carbohydrate, they would have been another important staple food and were eaten fresh or dried for soups or potage.

Pease porridge is mentioned in a Greek play written in 5 BC. Pease pudding, probably something similar, made with split peas with onion and herbs, is an old-fashioned but still very popular dish, especially in the north of England, traditionally eaten with ham and pork.

One of the first recipes for peas, however, comes from *Le Cuisinier Français*, which was translated into English in the middle of the seventeenth century and gives a recipe for *petits pois à la française* (peas cooked with small hearted lettuces) – still a popular recipe today.

Varieties

Mangetouts: These are eaten whole and have a delicate flavour, providing they are not overcooked. Unfortunately, they are easy to overcook and the texture then becomes rather slippery. Alternatively, blanch or stir-fry them. They are also good served raw in salads.

Petits Pois: These are not, as you might expect, immature peas but are a dwarf variety. Gardeners grow their own, but they are not available fresh in the shops as they are mainly grown commercially for canning or freezing.

Snow Peas, Sugar Peas, Sugar Snaps: These have the distinct fresh flavour of raw peas and are more plump and have more snap than mangetouts.

Buying and Storing

Only buy fresh peas; if they are old they are bound to be disappointing and you would be better off buying them frozen. In top condition, the pods are bright green and lively looking; the more withered the pod, the longer they have been hanging around. It is possible to surreptitiously sample peas on occasions, to check if they are fresh (greengrocers don't seem to mind if you buy some). Use fresh peas as soon as possible.

Preparing

Shelling peas can be very relaxing. Press open the pods and use your thumb to push out the peas *(below)*. Mangetouts and sugar snaps just need to be topped and tailed *(below right)*.

Left: Peas.
Above right: Sugar snap peas.

Cooking

Cook peas with a sprig of mint in a pan of rapidly boiling water or in a covered steamer until tender. Alternatively, melt butter in a flameproof casserole, add the peas and then cover and sweat over a gentle heat for 4–5 minutes. Cook mangetouts and sugar snaps in any of the same ways but for a shorter time.

GREEN BEANS

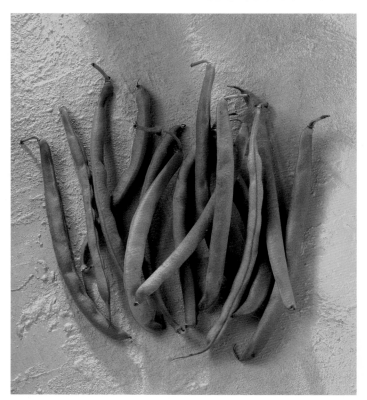

slim in shape. They should be eaten when very young, no more than 6-7.5cm/2½-3in in length.

Thai Beans: These long beans are similar to French beans and can be prepared and cooked in the same way.

Yellow Wax Beans: This is also a French bean and has a mild, slightly buttery taste.

Buying and Storing

Whatever variety, beans should be bright and crisp. Avoid wilted ones, or those with overly mature pods which feel spongy when lightly squeezed. They do not keep well, so use as soon as possible after buying or picking.

Preparing

To top and tail the beans: gather them together in one hand and then slice away the top 5mm/¼in *(below)*, then do the same at the other end. If necessary, pull off any stringy bits.

Whether you call beans French beans, wax beans, haricots or green beans, they all belong to a large and varied family.

History

The bean is a New World vegetable that had been cultivated for thousands of years by native people in both the north and south of the continent, which accounts for its wide diversity.

Varieties

One variety or another is available all year round and so they are one of the most convenient fresh green vegetables.

French Beans: This name encompasses a range of green beans, including the snap bean and bobby bean. They are mostly fat and fleshy and when fresh, should be firm so that they break in half with a satisfying snapping sound.

Haricots Verts: These are considered the best French beans and are delicate and

Cooking

Plunge beans into rapidly boiling salted water and cook until *al dente*. When overcooked, beans have a flabby texture and also lose much of their flavour. Drain and toss them in butter or serve in a sauce with shallots and bacon. For salads, cook until just tender and then refresh under cold water. They are excellent with a garlicky vinaigrette. Serve with carrots or other root vegetables and savour the contrast in flavours.

Above left: Bobby beans.
Below left: Yellow wax beans.
Right: Haricots verts.
Below: Thai beans.

SWEETCORN

Fresh sweetcorn, eaten on the cob with salt and a little butter is deliciously sweet. Some gardeners who grow it have a pan ready on the boil, so that when they cut the corn it goes into the pan in only the time it takes to race up from the garden to the kitchen. Buying it from the supermarket is inevitably a bit hit-or-miss, although if purchased in season, sweetcorn can be very good indeed.

History

In 1492, as Christopher Columbus disembarked on the island now called Cuba, he was met by American Indians offering two gifts of hospitality – one was tobacco and the other something the Indians called *maïs*. The English word for staple food was then corn, so that when Columbus and his crew saw that maize was the staple food for the Indians, it was dubbed "Indian corn".

Corn originated in South America and had enormous significance to the native Indians of the whole continent, who were said to have lived and died by corn. They referred to it as their "first mother and father, the source of life". By far their most important food, corn was used in many other ways as well. They used the plant for their shelters and for fences, and they wore it and decorated their bodies with it.

The Aztecs had corn planting ceremonies that included human sacrifices, and other tribes had similar customs to appease the god "corn". Countless myths and legends have been woven around corn, each tribe telling a slightly different story, but each on the same theme of planting and harvesting corn. For anthropologists and historians, they make compelling study.

Nutrition

Corn is a good carbohydrate food and is rich in vitamins A, B and C. It contains protein, but less so than most other cereals. It is also a good source of potassium, magnesium, phosphorus and iron.

Varieties

There are five main varieties of corn – popcorn, sweet corn, dent corn, flint corn and flour corn. Dent corn is the most commonly grown worldwide, for animal feeds and oil, and the corn we eat on the cobs is sweet corn. Baby sweetcorn cobs are picked when immature and are cooked and eaten whole.

Buying and Storing

As soon as corn is picked, its sugar begins to turn to starch and therefore the sooner it goes into the pot, the better. Wherever possible, buy locally grown sweetcorn.

Look for husks that are clean and green and tassels which are golden, with no sign of matting. The corn itself should look plump and yellow. Avoid cobs with pale or white kernels or those with older shrivelled kernels which will undoubtedly be disappointing.

Preparing

Strip away the husks. To use the kernels for recipes, cut downwards using a sharp knife from top to bottom *(left)*.

Cooking

Cook corn-on-the-cob in plenty of boiling salted water until tender. Timing depends on the size of the cobs but 10-15 minutes will normally be enough. Serve them with sea salt and butter, but if the cobs are really sweet, leave out the butter. Stir-fry baby sweetcorn cobs briefly and serve in oriental dishes.

Far left: Sweetcorn cobs.
Below: Baby sweetcorn cobs.

OKRA

History

Okra originated in Africa. In the sixteenth century, when African people were enslaved by the Spanish and shipped to the New World, they took with them the few things they could, including the plants and seeds from home – dried peas, yams, ackee – and okra. This lantern-shaped pod containing rows of seeds oozes a sticky mucilaginous liquid when cooked, and it was popular not only for its subtle flavour but also for thickening soups and stews.

The plant thrived in the tropical climate and by the early nineteenth century, when the slave trade was finally abolished, okra was an important part of the cuisine of the Caribbean and the southern United States. In and around New Orleans, the Creoles, the American-born descendants of European-born settlers, adopted a popular native American-Indian dish called *gumbo*. An essential quality of this famous dish was its thick gluey consistency. The Indians used filé powder (the dry pounded leaves of the sassafras tree), but okra was welcomed as a more satisfactory alternative.

Gumbos are now the hallmark of Creole cooking, and in some parts of America, the word "gumbo" is an alternative word for okra itself.

Buying and Storing

Choose young, small pods as older ones are likely to be fibrous. They should be bright green, firm and slightly springy when squeezed. Avoid any that are shrivelled or bruised. They will keep for a few days in the salad drawer of the fridge.

Preparing

When cooking whole, trim the top but don't expose the seeds inside or the viscous liquid will ooze into the rest of the dish. If, however, this is what you want, slice thickly or thinly according to the recipe *(right)*. If you want to eliminate some of this liquid, first soak the whole pods in acidulated water (water to which lemon juice has been added) for about an hour.

Cooking

The pods can be steamed, boiled or lightly fried, and then added to or used

with other ingredients. If cooked whole, okra is not mucilaginous but is pleasantly tender. Whether cooked whole or sliced, use garlic, ginger or chilli to perk up the flavour, or cook Indian-style, with onions, tomatoes and spices.

Above: Okra.

DRIED BEANS AND PEAS

Dried beans feature in traditional cuisines all over the world, from Mexican re-fried beans to Italy's *pasta e fagioli.* They are nutritious, providing a good source of protein when combined with rice, and are a marvellous store cupboard standby.

Black-eyed Beans: Sometimes called black-eyed peas, these small cream-coloured beans have a black spot or eye. When cooked, they have a tender, creamy texture and a mildly smoky flavour. Black-eyed beans are widely used in Indian cooking.

Chana Dhal: Chana dhal is very similar to yellow split peas but smaller in size and with a slightly sweeter taste. It is used in a variety of vegetable dishes.

Chick-peas: These round beige-coloured pulses have a strong, nutty flavour when cooked. As well as being used for curries, chick-peas are also ground into a flour which is widely used in many Indian dishes such as *pakoras* and *bhajees.*

Flageolet Beans: Small oval beans which are either white or pale green in colour. They have a very mild, refreshing flavour and feature in classic French dishes.

Green Lentils: Also known as continental lentils, these have quite a strong flavour and retain their shape during cooking. They are very versatile and are used in a number of dishes.

Haricot Beans: Small, white oval beans which come in different varieties. Haricot beans are ideal for Indian cooking because not only do they retain their shape but they also absorb the flavours of the spices.

Kidney Beans: Kidney beans are one of the most popular pulses. They are dark red/brown, kidney-shaped beans with a strong flavour.

Mung Beans: These are small, round green beans with a slightly sweet flavour and creamy texture. When sprouted they produce the familiar beansprouts.

Red Split Lentils: A readily available lentil that can be used for making dhal. Use instead of toovar dhal.

Toovar Dhal: A dull orange-coloured split pea with a very distinctive earthy flavour. Toovar dhal is available plain and in an oily variety.

Soaking and Cooking Tips

Most dried pulses, except lentils, need to be soaked overnight before cooking. Wash the beans thoroughly and remove any small stones and damaged beans. Put into a large bowl and cover with plenty of cold water. When cooking, allow double the volume of water to beans and boil for 10 minutes. This initial boiling period is essential to remove any harmful toxins. Drain, rinse and cook in fresh water. The cooking time for all pulses varies depending on the type and their freshness. Pulses can be cooked in a pressure cooker to save time. Lentils, on the whole, do not need soaking. They should be washed in several changes of cold water before being cooked.

Left: Clockwise from bottom right: Mung beans, Flageolet beans, Chick-peas, Haricot beans, Black-eyed beans, Kidney beans.
Above: Clockwise from top: Red split lentils, Green lentils, Toovar dhal, Chana dhal.

COURGETTES

Courgettes are the best loved of all the squashes as they are so versatile. They are quick and easy to cook and are succulent and tender with a delicate, unassuming flavour. Unlike other squashes, they are available all year round.

Vegetables taste best when eaten immediately after they have been picked, and this particularly applies to courgettes. They have a long season and are good to grow since the more you cut, the more the plants produce. Left unchecked, they turn into marrows.

Varieties

The courgette is classified as a summer squash, *cucurbita pepo*, along with marrows and pattypan squashes.

Courgettes: Sometimes called zucchini, courgettes are basically immature marrows. The word is a diminutive of the French *courge*, meaning marrow, and similarly zucchini means miniature *zucca*, Italian for gourd. Courgettes have a deep green skin, with firm pale flesh. The seeds and pith found in marrows have yet to form but are visible in more mature courgettes. Conversely, the prized baby courgettes have no suggestion of seeds or pith and the flesh is completely firm.

Yellow Courgettes: These are bright yellow and somewhat straighter than green courgettes. They have a slightly firmer flesh than green courgettes but are otherwise similar.

Pattypan Squashes: These little squashes look like tiny custard squashes. They can be pale green, yellow or white and have a slightly firmer texture than courgettes, but a similar flavour. They can be sliced and grilled in the same way as courgettes but, to make the most of their size and shape, steam them whole until tender.

Summer Crooknecks: Pale yellow with curves at the neck and a bumpy skin, crooknecks are prepared and cooked in the same way as courgettes.

Italian Courgettes: These very long, thin courgettes are grown in Italy. They are treated liked ordinary courgettes but are strictly a bottle gourd.

Buying and Storing

Courgettes should be firm with a glossy, healthy looking skin. Avoid any that feel squashy or generally look limp, as they will be dry and not worth using. Choose small courgettes whenever possible and buy in small quantities as needed.

Preparing

The tiny young courgettes need no preparation at all, and if they still have their flowers, so much the better. Other courgettes should be topped and tailed and then prepared according to the recipe, either sliced or slit for stuffing.

Cooking

Baby courgettes need little or no cooking. Steam them whole or just blanch them. Sliced larger courgettes can be steamed or boiled but take care that they do not overcook as they go soggy very quickly. Alternatively, grill, roast or fry them. Try dipping slices in a light batter and then shallow frying in a blend of olive and sunflower oil. To roast, place them in a ovenproof dish, scatter with crushed garlic and a few torn basil leaves and sprinkle with olive oil; then bake in a very hot oven until tender, turning the slices occasionally.

Top left: Pattypan squashes.
Far left: Baby courgettes.
Left: Yellow courgettes.
Right: Italian courgettes beside white and green courgettes.

MARROWS AND SUMMER SQUASHES

Vegetable marrow is classified as a summer squash yet it is rather the poor relation of squashes. Most of the edible flesh is water and at best it is a rather bland vegetable, with a slightly sweet flavour. At worst, it is insipid and if cooked to a mush (which isn't unheard of), it is completely tasteless.

Marrows can be stuffed, although it involves a lot of energy expended for very little reward; but marrow cooked over a low heat in butter with no added water (so that it steams in its own juice) brings out the best in it.

History

Marrows, like all the summer and winter squashes, are native to America. Squashes were eaten by native American-Indians, traditionally with corn and beans, and in an Iroquois myth the three vegetables are represented as three inseparable sisters. Although the early explorers would almost certainly have come into contact with them, they were not brought back home, and vegetable marrow was not known in England until the nineteenth century. Once introduced, however, it quickly became very popular. Mrs Beeton gives eight recipes for vegetable marrow and observes that "it is now extensively used". No mention at all is made of courgettes, which of course are simply immature marrows, as any gardener will know.

Varieties

The word "marrow" as a general term tends to refer to the summer squashes. At the end of summer and in the early autumn a good variety of the large summer squashes is available.

Vegetable Marrows: This is the proper name for the large prize marrows, beloved of harvest festivals and country fairs. Buy small specimens whenever possible.

Spaghetti Squashes/Marrows: Long and pale yellow, like all marrows these squashes can grow to enormous sizes, but buy small specimens for convenience as well as flavour. They earned their name from the resemblance of the cooked flesh to spaghetti.

To boil a spaghetti squash, first pierce the end, so that the heat can reach the middle, then cook for about 25 minutes or until the skin feels tender. Cut the squash in half lengthways, remove the seeds, and then fork the strands of flesh out on to a plate. It has a fragrant, almost honey and lemon flavour and tastes good with garlic butter or pesto.

Custard Marrows: These are pretty, pale green squashes with scalloped edges and a similar flavour to courgettes. If possible, buy small specimens, about 10cm/4in across. Boil these whole until tender, then cut a slice off the tops, scoop out the seeds and serve with a knob of butter.

Buying and Storing

Buy vegetables that have clear, unblemished flesh and avoid any with soft or brown patches. Vegetable marrows and spaghetti squashes will keep for several months provided they are kept in a cool, dark place. Custard marrows will keep up to a week.

Preparing

Wash the skin. For sautéing or steaming, or if the skin is tough, peel it away. For braised marrow, cut into chunks and discard the seeds and pith (*right*). For stuff-

ing, cut into thick slices or cut lengthways and discard the seeds and pith.

Cooking

Place chunks of marrow in a heavy-based pan with a little butter, cover and cook until tender. It can then be livened up with garlic, herbs or tomatoes. For stuffed marrow, blanch first, stuff, then cover or wrap it in foil to cook.

Above: Vegetable marrows.
Far left: Spaghetti squashes.
Left: Custard marrows.

PUMPKINS AND WINTER SQUASHES

Pumpkins are the most famous of the winter squashes; aesthetically they are one of nature's most pleasing vegetables for their huge size, their colour and the smoothness of their skin. They originally came from America and, from a culinary point of view, they have their home there.

The name squash comes from America and as well as pumpkins, the family includes acorn, butternut and turban squashes to name but a few. There are simply hundreds of different squashes, including Sweet Dumpling, Queensland Blue (from Australia), Calabaza, Cushaw and Golden Nugget.

History

The tradition of eating pumpkin at Thanksgiving came from when the Pilgrim Fathers, who had settled in New England, proclaimed a day of thanksgiving and prayer for the harvest. The early tradition was to serve the pumpkin with its head and seeds removed, the cavity filled with milk, honey and spices, and baked until tender. The custom of eating pumpkin at Thanksgiving has remained but it is now served in a different way: puréed pumpkin, either fresh or tinned, is used to make golden tarts.

Varieties

There are a huge number of varieties of winter squashes and, confusingly, many are known by several different names. However, from a cooking point of view, most are interchangeable although it is best to taste dishes as you cook them, as seasoning may differ from one to the other. In general, they all have a floury and slightly fibrous flesh and a mild, almost bland flavour tinged with sweetness. Because of this blandness, they harmonize well with other ingredients.

Acorn Squashes: These are small and heart-shaped with a beautiful deep green or orange skin, or a mixture of the two. Peel, then use as for pumpkins or bake whole, then split and serve with butter.

Butternut Squashes: Perfectly pear-shaped, these are a buttery colour. Use in soups or in any pumpkin recipe.

Delicata Squashes: This pretty pale yellow squash has a succulent yellow flesh,

tasting like a cross between sweet potato and butternut squash.

English Pumpkins: These have a softer flesh than the American variety and are good for soups or, if puréed, combined with potatoes or other root vegetables.

Hubbard Squashes: These large winter squashes have a thick, bumpy, hard shell which can range in colour from bright orange to dark green. If they are exceptionally large, they are sometimes sold in halves or large wedges. They have a grainy texture and are best mashed with butter and seasoning.

Kabocha Squashes: Attractive bright green squashes with a pale orange flesh.

They are similar in flavour and texture to acorn squashes and can be prepared and cooked in the same way.

Onion Squashes: Round, yellow or pale orange, onion squashes have a mild flavour, less sweet than pumpkin but still with a slightly fruity or honey taste. They are good in risottos or in most pumpkin recipes, but taste for flavour – you may need to add extra seasoning or sugar.

Above: Clockwise from right: A pumpkin hybrid, Kabocha squash, Acorn squash. Right: Clockwise from top right: Hybrid squash, two golden acorn squashes, two small and one large pumpkin.

Pumpkins: Large, bright yellow or orange squashes, with a deep orange flesh. They have a sweet, slightly honeyed, flavour and are very much a taste North Americans and Australians grow up with. However, they are not to everyone's liking and some people find them rather cloying. Pumpkin soup, pumpkin bread and pumpkin pie are part of the American tradition, as are faces carved from the shell at Hallowe'en.

Buying and Storing

All winter squashes may be stored for long periods. Buy firm, unblemished vegetables with clear smooth skins.

Preparing

For larger squashes, or for those being used for soups or purées, peel and cut into pieces, removing the seeds (*left*).

Cooking

Boil in a little water for about 20 minutes until tender, then mash and serve with butter and plenty of salt and pepper. Smaller squashes can be baked whole in their skins, then halved, seeded and served with butter and maple syrup. Pumpkin and other squashes can also be lightly sautéed in butter before adding stock, cream or chopped tomatoes.

EXOTIC GOURDS

While the squashes are native to America, most gourds originated in the Old World – from Africa, India and the Far East. However, over the millennia, seeds crossed water and, over the centuries, people crossed continents so that squashes and gourds are now common all over the world. Both belong to the family *Cucurbitacea,* and both are characterised by their rapid-growing vines.

Bottle Gourds: Bottle gourds are still a familiar sight in Africa, where they are principally grown not for their fruit, but for their dried shells. The gourds can grow to enormous sizes and the shells are used for water bottles, cups and musical instruments. The young fruit can be eaten, but it is extremely bitter and is normally only added to highly flavoured stews, like curries.

Chayotes: The chayote (pronounced chow-chow) is a popular gourd in all sorts of regions of the world and can be found in just about any ethnic supermarket, be it Chinese, African, Indian or Caribbean. In each it is known by a different name, christophine being the Caribbean term, but choko, shu-shu and chinchayote are among its many other names used elsewhere. Unlike most gourds, it originated in Mexico but was widely grown throughout the tropics after the invasions of the Spanish.

It is a pear-shaped fruit with a large central stone and has a cream-coloured or green skin. It has a bland flavour, similar to marrow, and a slightly firmer texture something like pumpkin. It is commonly used in Caribbean cooking, primarily as a side dish or in soufflés. Alternatively it can be used raw in salads.

Chinese Bitter Melons: These are a common vegetable in all parts of Asia and go by a myriad of names – bitter gourd and bitter cucumber to name but two. They are popular throughout Asia, eaten when very young, but are extremely bitter and rarely eaten in the West. They are easily recognized as they have warty, spiny skins, looking like a toy dinosaur. The skins are white when young but will probably have ripened to a dark green by the time they appear in the shops.

Most recipes from China suggest halving the gourd, removing the pulp and then slicing before boiling for several minutes to remove their bitterness. They can then be added to stir-fries or other oriental dishes.

Far left: Sweet dumpling.
Left: Pumpkin.
Top right: Chinese bitter melon.
Middle right: Loofah.
Below: Chayote.

Smooth and Angled Loofahs: The smooth loofah must be one of the strangest plants. When young it can be eaten, although it is not much valued. However, the plant is grown almost exclusively for sponges, used everywhere as a back rub in the bath. The ripe loofahs are picked and, once the skin has been stripped off and the seeds shaken out, allowed to dry. The plant then gradually dries to a fibrous skeleton and thence to bathrooms everywhere - so now you know!

Angled or ribbed loofahs are more commonly eaten but again are only edible when young as they become unpleasantly bitter when mature. They taste something like courgettes and are best cooked in a similar way, either fried in butter or cooked with tomatoes, garlic and oil.

CUCUMBERS

The Chinese say food should be enjoyed for its texture as well as flavour; cucumbers have a unique texture and refreshing cool taste. An afternoon tea with cucumber sandwiches, thinly sliced cucumber between wafer thin brown buttered bread, provides a delight of contrasts – the soft bread, the smooth butter and the cool crisp cucumber.

Varieties

English Cucumbers: These are the cucumbers the English are most familiar with. They have fewer seeds and thinner skin than the ridged cucumber.
Gherkins: These are tiny cucumbers with bumpy, almost warty skins and are mostly pickled in vinegar and eaten with cold meats or chopped into mayonnaise.
Kirbys: Small cucumbers, available in the United States and used for pickling.
Ridged Cucumbers: These are smaller than most cucumbers with more seeds and a thick, bumpy skin. You can buy them all over France but otherwise they tend to be available only in specialist greengrocers. The waxed ones need to be peeled before eating but most ridged cucumbers on the Continent are unwaxed and good without peeling.

Buying and Storing

Cucumbers should be firm from top to bottom. They are often sold pre-wrapped in plastic and can be stored in the salad drawer of the fridge for up to a week. Remove the plastic packaging once you've "started" a cucumber. Discard once it begins to go soggy.

Preparing

Whether you peel a cucumber or not is a matter of personal preference, but wash it if you don't intend to peel it. Some producers use wax coatings to give a glossy finish and these cucumbers must be peeled. If you are in doubt, buy organic cucumbers. Special citrus peelers can remove strips of peel to give an attractive striped effect when sliced.

Left: Cucumbers.
Above right: Ridged cucumbers.
Above far right: Baby cucumbers.
Below right: Kirbys.

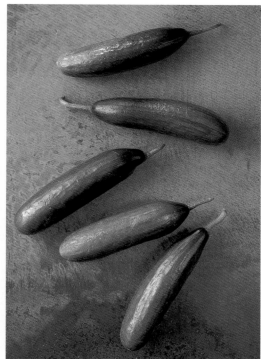

Serving

Thinly sliced cucumber is most frequently served with a light dressing or soured cream. In Greece cucumber is an essential part of a Greek country salad, *horiatiki salata*, cut into thick chunks and served with tomatoes, peppers and feta and dressed simply with olive oil and a little wine vinegar.

Iced cucumber soup is delicious, and cucumber can also be puréed with yogurt, garlic and herbs and served with soured cream stirred in.

Cooking

Cucumbers are normally served raw, but are surprisingly good cooked. Cut the cucumber into wedges, remove the seeds and then simmer for a few minutes until tender. Once drained, return the cucumber to the pan and stir in a little cream and seasoning.

TOMATOES

Next to onions, tomatoes are one of the most important fresh ingredients in the kitchen. In Mediterranean cooking, they are fundamental. Along with garlic and olive oil, they form the basis of so many Italian, Spanish and Provençal recipes that it is hard to find many dishes in which they are not included.

History

Tomatoes are related to potatoes, aubergines and sweet and chilli peppers, and all are members of the nightshade family. Some very poisonous members of this family may well have deterred our ancestors from taking to tomatoes. Indeed, the leaves of tomatoes are toxic and can result in very bad stomach aches.

Tomatoes are native to western South America. By the time of the Spanish invasions in the sixteenth century, they were widely cultivated throughout the whole of South America and Mexico. Hernán Cortés, conqueror of the Aztecs, sent the first tomato plants, a yellow variety, to Spain (no doubt along with the plundered Aztec gold).

However, people did not instinctively take to this "golden apple". English horticulturists mostly grew them as ornamental plants to adorn their gardens and had little positive to say about them as food. Spain is recorded as the first country to use tomatoes in cooking, stewing them with oil and seasoning. Italy followed suit, but elsewhere they were treated with suspicion.

The first red tomatoes arrived in Europe in the eighteenth century, brought to Italy by two Jesuit priests. They were gradually accepted in northern Europe where, by the mid-nineteenth century, they were grown extensively, eaten raw, cooked or used for pickles.

Above right: Red and yellow cherry tomatoes.
Below right: Yellow pear tomatoes.
Opposite above: Round or salad tomatoes on the vine.
Opposite below: Beefsteak tomatoes.

Varieties

There are countless varieties of tomatoes, ranging from the huge beef tomatoes that measure 10cm/4in across, to tiny cherry tomatoes, not much bigger than a thumb nail. They come in all shapes too - elongated, plum-shaped or slightly squarish and even pear-shaped.

Beefsteak Tomatoes: Large, ridged and deep red or orange in colour, these have a good flavour so are good in salads.

Canned Tomatoes: Keep a store of canned tomatoes, especially in the winter when fresh ones tend to taste insipid. Tomatoes are one of the few vegetables that take well to canning, but steer clear of any that are flavoured with garlic or herbs. It is far better to add flavouring yourself.

Cherry Tomatoes: These small, dainty tomatoes were once the prized treasures of gardeners but are now widely available. Although more expensive than round tomatoes, they have a delightful sweet flavour and are worth paying the

extra money for serving in salads or for cooking whole.

Plum Tomatoes: Richly flavoured with fewer seeds than regular tomatoes, these Italian-grown tomatoes are usually recommended for cooking, although they can be used in salads.

Round or Salad Tomatoes: These are the common tomatoes found in greengrocers and supermarkets. They vary in size according to the exact type and season. Sun-ripened tomatoes have the best flavour, however, for year-round availability the fruit is often picked and ripened off the plant. These tomatoes are versatile in everyday cooking. Adding a pinch of sugar and taking care to season the dish well helps to overcome any weakness in flavour.

Sun-Dried Tomatoes: This is one of the fashionable foods of the late Eighties and early Nineties. They add an evocative flavour to many Mediterranean dishes but don't use them too indiscriminately.

Tomato Purée: This is good for adding an intense tomato flavour, but use carefully or the flavour will be overpowering. Tubes have screw tops and are better than cans as, once they are opened, they can be kept for up to 4-6 weeks in the fridge.

Yellow Tomatoes: These are exactly like red tomatoes - they may be round, plum or cherry-sixed - except they are yellow.

Buying and Storing

Ideally, tomatoes should be allowed to ripen slowly on the plant so that their flavour can develop. Consequently, home-grown tomatoes are best, followed by those grown and sold locally. When buying from a supermarket or green-grocer, look at the leafy green tops; the fresher they look the better. Buy locally grown beefsteak or cherry tomatoes for salads and plum tomatoes for rich sauces. Paler tomatoes or those tinged with green will redden if kept in a brown paper bag or the salad drawer of the fridge, but if you intend to use tomatoes straight away, buy bright red speci-mens. Overripe tomatoes, where the skin has split and they seem to be bursting with juice, are excellent in soups. However, check for any sign of mould or decay, as this will spoil all your good efforts.

Preparing

Slice tomatoes across rather than down-wards for salads and pizza toppings. For wedges, cut downwards; halve or quarter and cut into two or three depending on the size of the tomato.

Cooking

Among the many classic tomato dishes is tomato soup, cooked to a delicate orange colour with stock or milk, or simmered with vegetables, garlic and basil. Recipes *à la provençale* indicate that tomatoes are in the dish; in Provençal cooking and Italian dishes, tomatoes are used with fish, meat and vegetables, in sauces and stuffings, with pasta and in superb salads. The Italian *tri colore salata* is a combination of large tomatoes, mozzarella and basil (the three colours of the Italian flag). The natural astringency of tomatoes means that, in salads, they need only be sprinkled with a fruity olive oil.

Chopped tomatoes add a depth of flavour to all sorts of meat and vegetarian dishes. Ideally, even in fairly rustic meals, the tomatoes should be peeled, since the skin can be irritating to eat once cooked. Some sauces also recom-mend seeding tomatoes, in which case cut the tomato into halves and scoop out the seeds before chopping (above).

Skinning Tomatoes

Cut a cross in the tops of the tomatoes, then place in a bowl and pour over boiling water. Leave for a minute (*above*), then use a sharp knife to peel away the skin, which should come away easily. Do a few at a time (five at most) otherwise they will begin to cook while soaking; boil the kettle for the next batch when you have finished peeling. The water must be boiling.

AUBERGINES

Many varieties of aubergines are cultivated and cooked all over the world. In Europe, Asia or America, they feature in a multitude of different dishes.

History

Although aubergines are a member of the nightshade family and thus related to potatoes, tomatoes and peppers, they were not discovered in the New World. The first mention of their cultivation is in China in 5 BC, and they are thought to have been eaten in India long before that. The Moors introduced the aubergine to Spain some 1200 years ago and it was grown in Andalucia. It is likely that they also introduced it to Italy, and possibly from there to other southern and eastern parts of Europe.

In spite of their popularity in Europe, aubergines did not become popular in Britain or the United States until very recently; although previous generations of food writers knew about them, they gave only the occasional recipe for cooking with them.

Above left: Plum tomatoes.
Top: Aubergines.
Above: Baby aubergines.
Left: Japanese aubergines.

Meanwhile, in the southern and eastern parts of Europe, aubergines had become extremely well liked, and today they are one of the most popular vegetables in the Mediterranean. Indeed, Italy, Greece and Turkey claim to have 100 ways of cooking them. In the Middle East, aubergines are also a central part of their cuisine.

Varieties

There are many different varieties of aubergines, differing in colour, size and shape according to their country of origin. Small ivory-white and plump aubergines look like large eggs (hence their name in the States: eggplant). Pretty striped aubergines may be either purple or pink and flecked with white irregular stripes. The Japanese or Asian aubergine is straight and very narrow, ranging in colour from a pretty variegated purple and white to a solid purple. It has a tender, slightly sweet flesh. Most aubergines, however, are either glossy purple or almost black and can be long and slim or fat like zeppelins. All aubergines have a similar flavour and texture; they taste bland yet slightly smoky when cooked, and the flesh is spongy to touch when raw, but soft after cooking.

Buying and Storing

Aubergines should feel heavy and firm to the touch, with glossy, unblemished skins. They will keep well in the salad drawer of the fridge for up to two weeks.

Preparing

When frying aubergines for any dish where they need slicing (e.g. ratatouille), it is a good idea to salt the slices first in order to draw out some of their moisture, otherwise, they absorb enormous quantities of oil during cooking (they absorb copious amounts anyway, but salting

reduces this slightly). Salting also used to be advised to reduce their bitterness but today's varieties are rarely bitter. To salt aubergines, cut into slices, about 1cm/¹/₂ in thick for fried slices, *(top right)* or segments *(above right)* and sprinkle generously with salt. Leave them to drain in a colander for about one hour, then rinse well and gently squeeze out the moisture from each slice or carefully pat dry with a piece of muslin.

Cooking

Aubergine slices can be fried in olive oil, as they are or first coated in batter – both popular Italian and Greek starters.

For moussaka, *parmigiana* and other dishes where aubergines are layered with other ingredients, fry the slices

briefly in olive oil. This gives them a tasty crust, while the inside stays soft.

To make a purée, such as for Poor Man's Caviar, first prick the aubergine all over with a fork and then roast in a moderately hot oven for about 30 minutes until tender. Scoop out the flesh and mix with spring onions, lemon juice and olive oil. One of the most famous aubergine dishes is *Imam Bayaldi* – "the Iman fainted" – fried aubergines stuffed with onions, garlic, tomato, spices and lots of olive oil.

Above left: White aubergines.
Below left: Striped aubergines.
Above: Thai aubergines, including white, yellow and Pea aubergines.

PEPPERS

In spite of their name, peppers have nothing to do with the spice pepper used as a seasoning, although early explorers may have been mistaken in thinking the fruit of the shrubby plant looked like the spice they were seeking. It is thanks to this 400-year-old mistake that the name "pepper" has stuck.

History

The journeys Christopher Columbus and the conquistadors made were partly to find the spices Marco Polo had found a hundred years earlier in the Far East. Instead of the Orient, however, Columbus discovered the Americas, and instead of spices, he found maize, potatoes and tomatoes. He would have noted, though, that the American-Indians flavoured their food with ground peppers, and since it was hot, like pepper, perhaps wishful thinking coloured his objectivity. In any case, he returned with the new vegetables, describing them as peppers and advertising them as more pungent than those from Caucasus.

Varieties

Peppers and chillies are both members of the capsicum family. To distinguish between them, peppers are called sweet peppers, bell peppers and even bullnose peppers and come in a variety of colours – red, green, yellow, white, orange and a dark purple-black.

The colour of the pepper tells you something about its flavour. Green peppers are the least mature and have a fresh "raw" flavour. Red peppers are ripened green peppers and are distinctly sweeter. Yellow/orange peppers taste more or less like red peppers, although perhaps slightly less sweet and if you have a fine palate you may be able to detect a difference. Black peppers have a similar flavour to green peppers but when cooked are a bit disappointing as they turn green; so if you buy them for their dramatic colour, they are best used in salads.

In Greece and other parts of southern Europe, longer, slimmer peppers are often available which have a more pronounced sweet and pungent flavour than the bell-shaped peppers – although this may be because they are locally picked and therefore absolutely fresh. Whichever is the case, they are quite delicious.

Buying and Storing

Peppers should look glossy and sprightly and feel hard and crisp; avoid any that look wrinkled or have damp soft patches. They will keep for a few days at the bottom of the fridge.

Preparing

To prepare stuffed peppers, cut off the top and then cut away the inner core and pith, and shake out the seeds. The seeds and core are easily removed when halving, quartering or slicing.

Cooking

There are countless ways of cooking peppers. Sliced, they can be fried with onions and garlic in olive oil and then braised with tomatoes and herbs. This is the basic ratatouille; other vegetables, such as courgettes and aubergines, can of course be added.

Peppers can be roasted, either with ratatouille ingredients or with only onions and garlic. Cut into large pieces, place in a roasting pan and sprinkle with olive oil, torn basil and seasoning. Roast in a very hot oven (220°C/425°F/Gas 7) for about 30 minutes, turning occasionally. Grilled peppers are another superb dish. Once grilled they can be skinned to reveal a soft, luxurious texture and added to salads.

Above far left: Red, green and orange peppers.
Below far left: Yellow peppers.
Above left: White peppers.
Above right: Purple peppers.

Skinning Peppers

Cut the pepper into quarters lengthways and grill, skin side up (*above*), until the skin is charred and evenly blistered. Place the pieces immediately into a plastic bag (you will need tongs or a fork as they will be hot) and close the top of the bag with a tie or a loose knot. Leave for a few minutes and then remove from the bag and the skin will peel off easily.

CHILLIES

Some people apparently become so addicted to the taste of hot food that they carry little jars of chopped dried chillies around with them and scatter them over every meal. Although this is a bit extreme, it is chillies more than any other ingredient that spice up our mealtimes.

Varieties

Chillies are the most important seasoning in the world after salt. Unlike peppers, to which they are closely related, the different varieties of chilli can have widely different heat values – from the "just about bearable" to the "knock your head off" variety.

Anaheim Chilli: A long, thin chilli with a blunt end, named after the Californian city. It can be red or green and has a mild, sweet taste.

Ancho Chilli/Pepper: These look like tiny peppers. They are mild enough to taste their underlying sweetness.

Birdseye or Bird Chilli: These small red chillies are fiery hot. Also known as pequin chillies.

Cayenne Pepper: This is made from the dried, ground seeds and pods of chillies. The name comes from the capital of French Guiana, north of Brazil, although the cayenne chilli does not grow there any longer and the pepper is made from chillies grown all over the world.

Early Jalapeño: A popular American chilli, which starts dark green and gradually turns to red.

Habañero: Often called Scotch Bonnet, this is the hottest of all chillies and is small and can be green, red or yellow. Colour is no real guide to its heat properties, so don't be fooled into thinking that green ones are mild. They are all *very* hot. The habàñero comes from Mexico and is frequently used in Mexican and Caribbean dishes.

Hot Gold Spike: A large, pale, yellow-green fruit grown in the south-western United States: it is very hot.

Above: Birdseye chillies.
Left: Habañero chillies (in and below bowl) and Yellow wax peppers.

Preparing

The capsaicin in chillies is most concentrated in the pith inside the pod and this, together with the seeds, should be cut away (*below*) unless you want maximum heat. Capsaicin irritates the skin and especially the eyes, so take care when preparing chillies. Either wear gloves or wash your hands thoroughly after handling chillies. If you rub your eyes, even if you have washed your hands carefully, it will be painful.

Poblano: A small, dark green chilli, served whole in Spain either roasted or grilled. They are mostly mild but you can get the rogue fiery one, so beware if eating them whole.

Red Chilli: These are long, rather wrinkled chillies which are green at first and then gradually ripen to red. They are of variable hotness and, because they are so long and thin, are rather fiddly to prepare.

Serrano Chilli: A long, red and extremely hot chilli.

Tabasco: A sauce made with chillies, salt and vinegar and first made in New Orleans. It is a fiery sauce, popular in Creole, Caribbean and Mexican cookery – or indeed in any dish requiring last minute heat.

Yellow Wax Pepper: Pale yellow to green, these can vary from mild to hot.

Buying and Storing

Some fresh chillies look wrinkled even in their prime and therefore this is not a good guide to their freshness. They should, however, be unblemished, and avoid any which are soft or bruised.

The substance which makes the chilli hot is a volatile oil called capsaicin. This differs not only from one type to another but also from plant to plant, depending on growing conditions; the more the plant has to struggle to survive in terms of light, water, soil, etc, the more capsaicin will be produced. It is therefore impossible to tell how hot a chilli will be before tasting, although some types are naturally hotter than others. The belief that green chillies are milder than red ones does not necessarily follow; generally red chillies will have ripened for longer in the sun with the result that they will only be sweeter for all that sunshine.

Chillies can be stored in a plastic bag in the fridge for a few days.

Cooking

In Mexican cooking chillies play a vital, and almost central role. It is difficult to think of any savoury Mexican dish that does not contain either fresh chillies or some form of processed chilli, whether canned, dried or ground. Other cuisines, however, are equally enthusiastic about chillies. They are essential in curries and similar dishes from India and the Far East, and in Caribbean and Creole food they are also used extensively.

If you have developed a tolerance for really hot food, then there is no reason why you shouldn't add as many as you wish. In general, however, use chillies discreetly, if for no better reason than you can't take the heat away if you make a mistake.

Above: Ancho chillies (left) and Anaheim chillies (on board).

Plantains and Green Bananas

While bananas are well and truly fruit, eaten almost exclusively as a dessert or by themselves as fruit, plantains can reasonably be considered among the vegetable fraternity as they have a definite savoury flavour, are normally eaten as a first or main course and can only be eaten once cooked.

Varieties

Plantains: Also known as cooking bananas, these have a coarser flesh and more savoury flavour than sweet bananas. While superficially they look exactly like our own bananas, they are, on closer inspection, altogether larger and heavier looking. They can vary in colour from the unripe fruit, which is green, through yellow to a mottled black colour, which is when the fruit is completely ripe.

Green Bananas: Only certain types of green bananas are used in African and Caribbean cooking, and the "greenish" bananas you find in most western supermarkets are normally eating bananas, just waiting to ripen. If you need green bananas for a recipe, look out for them in West Indian or African cookshops.

Preparing

Plantains: These are inedible raw and must be cooked before eating. Unless very ripe, the skin can be tricky to remove. With yellow and green plantains, cut the fruit into short lengths, then slit the skin along the natural ridge of each piece of plantain. Gently ease the skin away from the flesh and pull the skin until it peels off completely (*below*).

Once peeled, plantains can be sliced horizontally or into lengths and then roasted or fried. Like bananas, plantains will discolour if exposed to the air so, if not using immediately, sprinkle with lemon juice or place in a bowl of salted water.

Green Bananas: These should be prepared in a similar way. As with plantains, green bananas should not be eaten raw and are usually boiled, either in their skins or not, according to the recipe.

If making green banana crisps, use a potato peeler to produce the thinnest slices (*left*).

If cooking plantains or green bananas in their skins, slit the skin lengthways along the sides and place in a saucepan of salted water. Bring to the boil, simmer gently for about 20 minutes until tender and then cool. The peel can then easily be removed before slicing.

Cooking and Serving

Plantains and green bananas both have an excellent flavour. In many African and Caribbean recipes they are roasted or fried and then served simply with salt. However, if boiled, they can be sliced and served in a simple salad with a few sliced onions, or added to something far more elaborate like a gado gado salad, with mango, avocado, lettuce and prawns.

Plantains also make a delicious soup, where they are often teamed with sweetcorn. After frying an onion and a little garlic, add two sliced and peeled plantains, together with tomatoes, if liked. Fry gently for a few minutes and then add vegetable stock to cover and one or two sliced chillies, together with about 175g/6oz sweetcorn. Simmer gently together until the plantain is tender.

Above left: Plantains.
Below left: Green bananas.
Below: Canned ackee.

ACKEE

Ackee is a tropical fruit which is used in a variety of savoury dishes, mainly of Caribbean origin, where the fruit is very popular. The fruit itself is bright red and, when ripe, bursts open to reveal three large black seeds and a soft, creamy flesh resembling scrambled eggs. It has a slightly lemony flavour and is traditionally served with saltfish to make one of Jamaica's national dishes. Only buy ripe fruit as, when under-ripe, certain parts of the fruit are toxic.

However, unless you are visiting the Caribbean you are probably only likely to find ackee in cans, and indeed most recipes call for canned ackee which is a good substitute for the fresh fruit.

Jamaican cooks also use ackee to add a subtle flavour to a variety of vegetable and bean dishes. The canned ackee needs very little cooking, and should be added to dishes in the last few minutes of cooking. Take care when stirring into a dish as it breaks up very easily.

AVOCADOS

The avocado has been known by many names – butter pear and alligator pear to name but two. It earned the title butter pear clearly because of its consistency, but alligator pear was the original Spanish name. Although you would be forgiven for thinking this was due to its knobbly skin (among some varieties anyway), the name in fact derives from the Spanish which was based on the Aztec word, the basically unpronounceable *ahuacatl.* From this to the easily-said alligator and thence to avocado was but one short step.

History

The avocado is a New World fruit, native to Mexico, but while it would have been "discovered" by the Old World explorers, it didn't become a popular food in Europe until the middle of this century, when modern transport meant that growers in California, who started farming avocados in the middle of the nineteenth century, could market this fruit worldwide. Avocados are now also exported by South Africa and Australia.

Nutrition

The avocado is high in protein and carbohydrate. It is one of the few fruits that contains fat, and it is also rich in potassium, Vitamin C, some B vitamins and Vitamin E. Its rich oils, particularly its Vitamin E content, mean that it is not only useful as food, but for skin and hair

care too, something the Aztecs and Incas were aware of a thousand years ago. The cosmetic industry may have been in its infancy, but it still knew a good thing when it saw it.

Because of their valuable protein and vitamin content, avocados are a popular food for babies. They are easily blended, and small children generally enjoy their creamy texture and pleasant flavour.

Varieties

There are four varieties: Hass, the purple-black small knobbly avocado, the Ettinger and Fuerte, which are pear-shaped and have smooth green skin, and the Nabal, which is rounder in shape. The black-coloured Hass has golden-yellow flesh, while green avocados have pale green to yellow flesh.

Buying and Storing

The big problem in buying avocados is that they're never ripe when you want them to be. How often do you see shoppers standing by the avocado shelves, feeling around for that rare creature, the perfectly ripe avocado? Most times they all feel as hard as rocks; that or else they're hopelessly soft and squashy and clearly past their best. The proper and sensible thing to do is buy fruit a few days before you need it. An unripe avocado will ripen in between 4-7 days at room temperature. Once it is ripe, it will keep well in the fridge for a few days, but you still need to plan well in advance if you want to be sure of the perfect avocado.

The alternative is to hope for the best and keep feeling around until you find a ripe fruit. A perfect avocado should have a clean, unblemished skin without any brown or black patches. If ripe, it should "give" slightly if squeezed gently in the hand, but not so much that it actually feels soft. Over-ripe avocados are really not worth bothering with, however persuasive and generous the offer from the man on the market. The flesh will be unattractively brown and stringy and the bits of good flesh you do manage to salvage will be soft and pulpy. Good for a dip, but nothing much else.

Preparing

Although they are simple fruits, avocados can be the devil to prepare. Once peeled, you are left with a slippery object which is then almost impossible to remove from the stone.

If you intend to eat the avocados in halves, it's fairly simple to just prise out the stone once halved. If you want to slice the fruit, use this tip I learnt from my chef friend. The only thing you need is a very sharp knife. Cut the avocado in half, remove the stone and then, with the skin still on, cut through the flesh and the skin to make slices. It is then relatively simple to strip off the peel.

Remember to sprinkle the slices with lemon juice as the flesh discolours once exposed to the air.

Cooking

Most popular raw, avocados can also be baked, grilled or used in sautéed and sauced dishes.

Serving Ideas

As well as prawns or vinaigrette, a half avocado can hold a mixture of chopped tomatoes and cucumber, a mild garlic cheese dip or a soured cream potato salad. Slices of avocado are delicious served with sliced tomatoes and mozzarella, sprinkled simply with olive oil, lemon juice and plenty of black pepper. Avocado can be chopped and added to a salad, or puréed for a rich dressing.

In Mexico, where avocados grow in abundance, there are countless avocado recipes. Guacamole is perhaps the best known, but they are also eaten in soups and stews and commonly used to garnish tacos and enchiladas.

BREADFRUIT

Breadfruit is the name for a tropical tree that grows on the islands of the South Pacific ocean. The fruit of the tree is about the size of a small melon with a rough rind and a pale, mealy flesh.

Preparing

The fruit should be peeled and the core removed.

Cooking

Breadfruit can be treated like potatoes: the flesh may be boiled, baked or fried. It is a staple food for the people of the Pacific islands who bake the flesh, or dry and grind it for biscuits, bread and puddings. It has a sweet flavour and soft texture when ripe.

Left: Clockwise from the right: Fuerte, Hass and Nabal avocados.
Right: Breadfruit.

EIGHT

SALAD
VEGETABLES

Lettuce

Rocket

Chicory and Radicchio

Radishes

Watercress

Mustard and Cress

LETTUCE

One aspect of lettuce that sets it apart from any other vegetable is that you can only buy it in one form – fresh.

History

Lettuce has been cultivated for thousands of years. In Egyptian times it was sacred to the god Min, and tubs of lettuce were ceremoniously carried before this fertility god. It was then considered a powerful aphrodisiac, yet for the Greeks and the Romans lettuce was thought to have quite the opposite effect, making one sleepy and generally soporific. Chemists today confirm that lettuce contains a hypnotic similar to opium, and in herbal remedies lettuce is recommended for insomniacs.

Varieties

There are hundreds of different varieties of lettuce. Today, an increasing variety is available in the shops so that the salad bowl can be wealth of colour and texture.

Round Lettuces

Sometimes called head or cabbage lettuces, round lettuces have cabbage-like heads and include:
Butterheads: These are the classic lettuces seen in kitchen gardens. They have a pale heart and floppy, loosely packed leaves. They have a pleasant flavour as long as they are fresh.
Crispheads: Crisp lettuces, such as Iceberg, have an excellent crunchy texture and will keep their vitality long after butterheads have faded and died.
Looseheads: These are non-hearting lettuce with loose leaves and include *lollo rosso* and *lollo biondo*, oakleaf lettuce and Red Salad Bowl. Although they are not particularly remarkable for their flavour, they look superb.

Cos Lettuces

The cos is the only lettuce that would have been known in antiquity. It is known

Above: Butterhead lettuce.
Right: Lollo rosso lettuce.
Above far right: Cos lettuce.
Below far right: Lamb's lettuce.
Below extreme right: Little Gem.

by two names: cos, derived from the Greek island where it was found by the Romans; and romaine, the name used by the French after it was introduced to France from Rome. There are two cos lettuces, both with long, erect heads.

Cos: Considered the most delicious lettuce, this has a firm texture and a faintly nutty texture. It is the correct lettuce for Caesar Salad, one of the classic salads.

Little Gems: In appearance Little Gems look like something between a baby cos and a tightly furled butterhead. They have firm hearts and are enjoyed for their distinct flavour. Like other lettuce hearts, they cope well with being cooked.

LAMB'S LETTUCE OR CORN SALAD

This popular winter leaf does not actually belong to the lettuce family (it is related to Fuller's teasel), but as it makes a lovely addition to salads, this seems a good place to include it. Called *mâche* in France, it has spoon-shaped leaves and an excellent nutty flavour.

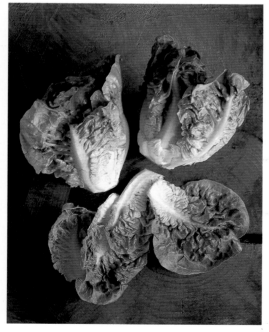

Nutrition

As well as containing vitamins A, C and
E, lettuce provides potassium, iron and
calcium and traces of other minerals.

Buying and Storing

The best lettuce is that fresh from the
garden. The next best thing is to buy lettuce from a farm shop or pick-your-own
(although if fertilizers and pesticides are
used, their flavour will be disappointing
compared to the organic product).
Nowadays, lettuce is frequently sold
ready shredded and packed with herbs
etc, an acceptable and convenient form
of buying lettuce. Whether you buy lettuce prepacked or from the shelf, it must
be fresh. Soil and bugs can be washed
off but those with limp or yellow leaves
are of no use. Eat lettuce as soon as possible after purchasing; in the meantime
keep it in a cool dark place, such as the
salad drawer of the fridge.

Making Salads

Salads can be made using only one lettuce or a mixture of many. There are no
rules but, when mixing salads, choose
leaves to give contrast in texture and
colour as well as flavour. Fresh herbs,
such as parsley, coriander and basil also
add an interesting dimension.

Tear rather than cut the leaves of loose-
leafed lettuce; icebergs and other large
lettuces are commonly sliced or shredded. Eat as soon as possible after
preparing.

Dressings should be well-flavoured with
a hint of sharpness but never too
astringent. Make them in a blender, a
screw top jar or in a large bowl so that
the ingredients can be thoroughly
blended. Always use the best possible
oils and vinegars, in roughly the proportion of five oil to one vinegar or lemon
juice. Use half good olive oil and half
sunflower oil, or for a more fragrant
dressing, a combination of walnut oil and
sunflower oil. A pinch of salt and pepper
is essential, French mustard is optional
and the addition of a little sugar will
blunt the flavour.

Add the dressing to the salad when
you're ready to serve – never before.

ROCKET

Rocket has a wonderful peppery flavour and is excellent in a mixed green salad. It has small, bright green dandelion-shaped leaves. The Greeks and Romans commonly ate rocket (*arugula*) in mixed salads, apparently to help counterbalance the dampening effect lettuce had on the libido – rocket's aphrodisiac properties in antiquity are well catalogued. It used to be sown around the statues of Priapus, the mythological Greek god of fertility and protector of gardens and herbs and son of Aphrodite and Dionysus.

Buying and Storing

Rocket is to be found either among the salads or fresh herbs in supermarkets. Buy fresh green leaves and use soon after purchasing. If necessary, the leaves can be kept immersed in cold water.

Preparing and Serving

Discard any discoloured leaves. Add rocket to plain green salads, or grind with garlic, pine nuts and olive oil for a dressing for pasta.

Since it has such a striking flavour, a little rocket goes a long way, making it an excellent leaf for garnishing. It tastes superb contrasted with grilled goat's cheese, or one or two leaves can be added to sandwiches, or loosely packed into pitta bread pockets along with tomatoes, avocado, peanuts and bean sprouts.

Above left: Oak Leaf lettuce.
Below left: Curly endive.
Below: Rocket.

RADISHES

Radishes have a peppery flavour that can almost be felt in the nostrils as you bite into one. Their pungency depends not only on the varieties but also on the soil in which they are grown. Freshly harvested radishes have the most pronounced flavour and crisp texture.

Varieties

Radishes were loved throughout antiquity and consequently there are many varieties worldwide. Both the small red types and the large white radishes are internationally popular.

Red Radishes: These small red orbs have many pretty names, such as Cherry Belle and Scarlet Globe, but are mostly sold simply as radish. They are available all year round, have a deep pink skin, sometimes paler or white at the roots and a firm white flesh. Their peppery flavour is milder in the spring and they are almost always eaten raw. Finely sliced and sandwiched in bread and butter, they make an interesting *hors d'oeuvre*.

French Breakfast Radishes: These are red and white and slightly more elongated than the red radish. They tend to be milder than English radishes and are popular in France either eaten on their own or served with other raw vegetables as *crudités*.

Mooli or Daikon Radishes: Sometimes known as the oriental radish, the mooli is a smooth-skinned, long, white radish. Those bought in the shops have a mild flavour, less peppery than the red radish – perhaps because they lose their flavour after long storage (moolis straight from the garden are hot and peppery). They can be eaten raw or pickled, or added to stir-fries.

Buying and Storing

Buy red radishes that are firm with crisp leaves. If at all possible, buy moolis or daikons which still have their leaves; this is a good indication of their freshness as they wilt quickly. The leaves should be green and lively and the skins clear with no bruises or blemishes. They can be stored in the fridge for a few days.

Preparing and Serving

Red radishes need only to be washed. They can then be sliced or eaten whole by themselves or in salads. You can make a feature of them by slicing into a salad of, say, oranges and walnuts, perhaps with a scattering of rocket and dressed with a walnut oil vinaigrette. To use moolis in a stir-fry, cut into slices and add to the dish for the last few minutes of cooking. They add not only flavour but also a wonderfully juicy and crunchy texture.

Left: Red radishes.
Above: French breakfast radishes.
Right: Mooli or daikon radishes.

WATERCRESS

Watercress is perhaps the most robustly flavoured of all the salad ingredients and a handful of watercress is all you need to perk up a rather dull green salad. It has a distinctive "raw" flavour, both peppery and slightly pungent and this, together with its bright green leaves, make it a popular garnish.

Watercress, as the name suggests, grows in water. It needs fast flowing clean water to thrive and is really only successful around freshwater springs on chalk hills. The first watercress beds were cultivated in Europe but the vegetable is now grown worldwide.

WINTER CRESS

Winter cress or land cress is often grown as an alternative to watercress, when flowing water is not available. It looks like a robust form of watercress and indeed has a similar if even more assertive flavour, with a distinct peppery taste. Use as you would use watercress, either in salads or in soups.

Nutrition

Watercress is extremely rich in vitamins A, B2, C, D and E. It is also rich in calcium, potassium and iron and provides significant quantities of sulphur and chloride.

Buying and Storing

Only buy fresh looking watercress – the darker and larger the leaves the better. Avoid any with wilted or yellow leaves. It will keep for several days in the fridge or better still, submerged in a bowl, or arranged in a jar of cold water, and kept in a cool place.

Preparing and Cooking

Discard any yellow leaves and remove thick stalks which will be too coarse for salads or soups. Small sprigs can be added to salads.

For soups and purées, either blend watercress raw or cook briefly in stock, milk or water. Cooking inevitably destroys some of the nutrients but cooked watercress has a less harsh flavour, while still retaining its characteristic peppery taste.

MUSTARD <u>AND</u> CRESS

Mustard and cress are often grown together, to provide spicy greenery as a garnish or for salads. They are available all year round.

Mustard seedlings germinate 3-4 days sooner than the cress, so if you buy mustard and cress from the supermarket, or grow your own on the windowsill, initially the punnets will only show mustard seedlings.

History

Cress has been grown for thousands of years, known first to the Persians. There is a story that the Persians would always eat cress before they baked bread, and there are other references in antiquity to people eating cress with bread.

Serving

Today mustard and cress are often enjoyed in sandwiches, either served simply on buttered bread, or with avocado or cucumber added. Cress probably wouldn't be substantial enough as a salad in itself, but, with its faint spicy flavour, it can perk up a plain green salad, and it is also excellent in a tomato salad, dressed simply with olive oil and tarragon vinegar.

Above left: Watercress.
Below left: Winter cress.
Above right: Mustard seedlings.
Right: Cress seedlings.

MUSHROOMS

Button Mushrooms

Field Mushrooms

Woodland Mushrooms

Wild Mushrooms
and Other Fungi

BUTTON MUSHROOMS

There is nothing like fried mushrooms on toast for breakfast, served sizzling hot straight from the pan. Once cooked, mushrooms, especially fried ones, go soft and flabby quite quickly; they still taste OK but the pleasure is not so great.

History

In the past, mushrooms have had a firm association with the supernatural and even today their connection with the mysterious side of life hasn't completely disappeared. Fairy rings – circles of mushrooms – inexplicably appear overnight in woods and fields and thunder is still thought to bring forth fresh crops of mushrooms.

Many types of mushrooms and fungi are either poisonous or hallucinogenic, and in the past their poisons have been distilled for various murderous reasons.

The use of the term mushroom to mean edible species, and toadstool to mean those considered poisonous, has no scientific basis, and there is no simple rule for distinguishing between the two. Picking wild mushrooms is not safe unless you are confident about identifying edible types. In France, during the autumn, people take the wild mushrooms they have gathered to the local pharmacy for identification.

Varieties

Button/White Mushrooms: Cultivated mushrooms are widely available in shops and are sold when very young and tiny as button mushrooms. The slightly larger ones are known as closed cap, while larger ones still are open capped or open cup mushrooms. They have ivory or white caps with pinky/beige gills which darken as they mature. All have a pleasant unassuming flavour.

Chestnut Mushrooms: These have a thicker stem and a darker, pale brown cap. They have a more pronounced "mushroomy" flavour and a meatier texture than white mushrooms.

Buying and Storing

It is easy to see whether or not button mushrooms are fresh – their caps will be clean and white, without bruises or blemishes. The longer they stay on the shelves, the darker and more dis-coloured the caps become, while the gills underneath turn from pink to brown.

If possible, use the paper bags provid-ed in many supermarkets nowadays when buying mushrooms. Mushrooms in plastic bags sweat in their own heat, eventually turning slippery and unappe-tizing. If you have no choice or you buy mushrooms in cellophane-wrapped cartons, transfer loose to the bottom of the fridge as soon as possible. They will keep only for a day or two.

Preparing

Mushrooms should not be washed but wiped with a damp cloth or a piece of kitchen paper (*below*). This is partly because you don't want to increase their water content, and also because they should be fried as dry as possible.

Unless the skins are very discoloured, it should not be necessary to peel them, although you probably will need to trim the very base of the stem.

Cooking

Mushrooms are largely composed of water and shrink noticeably during cook-ing. They also take up a lot of fat as they cook so it is best to use butter or a good olive oil for frying. Fry mushrooms briskly over a moderately high heat so that as they shrink the water evaporates and they don't stew in their own juice. For the same reason do not fry too many mush-rooms at once in the same pan.

Most of the recipes in this book use fried mushrooms as their base and they are completely interchangeable – so if you can't get wild mushrooms or chestnut mushrooms for instance, button mush-rooms can be used instead.

Above: Button mushrooms.
Top right: Flat mushrooms.
Far right: Field mushrooms.
Right: Chestnut mushrooms (top) and open capped or cup mushrooms.

FIELD MUSHROOMS

Field mushrooms are the wild relatives of the cultivated mushroom and when cooked have a wonderful aroma. Flat mushrooms, although indistinguishable from field mushrooms in appearance, have probably been cultivated and are also excellent. Connoisseurs say that only wild mushrooms have any flavour but many would argue against this. However, if you know where to find field mushrooms, keep the secret to yourself (most mushroom devotees seem to know this) and count yourself lucky!

Buying and Storing

Field mushrooms are sometimes available during the autumn in farm shops. Since they are likely to have been picked recently, they should be fresh unless obviously wilting. Unless you intend to stuff them, don't worry if they are broken in places as you will be slicing them anyway. Use as soon as possible after purchase.

Preparing

Trim the stalk bottoms if necessary and wipe the caps with a damp cloth. Slice according to the recipe.

Cooking

For true field mushrooms, you need do nothing more complicated than simply fry them in butter or olive oil with a suggestion of garlic if liked. However, like flat mushrooms, field mushrooms can be used for stuffing, in soups or indeed any mushroom recipe. They are darker than button mushrooms and will colour soups and sauces brown, but the flavour will be extremely good.

When stuffing mushrooms, gently fry the caps on both sides for a few minutes. The stalks can be chopped and added to the stuffing or can be used for soups or stocks.

WOODLAND MUSHROOMS

Varieties

Ceps: Popular in France, where they are known as *cèpes* and in Italy where they are called *porcini*, these meaty, bun-shaped mushrooms have a fine almost suede-like texture and a good flavour. Instead of gills they have a spongy texture beneath the cap and unless they are very young it is best to scrape this away as it goes soggy when cooked. Ceps are excellent fried in oil or butter over a brisk heat to evaporate the liquid and then added to omelettes.

Alternatively, an Italian way of cooking is to remove the stalk and the spongy tubes, and brush the tops with olive oil. Grill for about 10 minutes under a moderate grill and then turn them over and pour olive oil and a sprinkling of garlic into the centre. Grill for a further 5 minutes and then serve sprinkled with seasoning and parsley.

Chanterelles: Frilly, trumpet-shaped chanterelles are delicate mushrooms which range in colour from cream to a vivid yellow. Later, winter chanterelles, have greyish-lilac gills on the underside of their dark caps. Chanterelles have a delicate, slightly fruity flavour and a firm, almost rubbery texture. They are difficult to clean as their tiny gills tend to trap grit and earth. Rinse them gently under cold running water and then shake dry. Fry in butter over a gentle heat to start with so they exude their liquid and then increase the heat to boil it off. They are delicious with scrambled eggs, or served by themselves with finely cut toast.

Horn of Plenty/Black Trumpets: Taking its name from its shape, this mushroom ranges in colour from mid-brown to black. As it is hollow, it will need to be brushed well to clean or, if a large specimen, sliced in half. It is very versatile, but goes particularly well with fish.

Morels: These are the first mushroom of the year, appearing not in autumn but in spring. In Scandinavia they are called the "truffles of the north" and are considered among the great edible fungi. They are cone-shaped with a crinkled spongy cap but are hollow inside. You will need to wash them well under running water as insects tend to creep into their dark crevices. Morels need longer cooking than most mushrooms: sauté them in butter, add a squeeze of lemon and then cover and simmer for up to an hour until tender. The juices can then be thickened with cream or egg yolks.

Dried Mushrooms: Most wild mushrooms are available dried. To reconstitute, soak in warm water for about 20-30 minutes; in the case of morels when they are added to stews, soak for about 10 minutes. Dried wild mushrooms, particularly ceps, have an intense flavour.

Left: Clockwise from the top: Ceps, Horn of Plenty, Chanterelles.
Above right: Dried mushrooms.
Above left: Morels.
Right: Winter chanterelles.

WILD MUSHROOMS AND OTHER FUNGI

Mushroom gathering, a seasonal event throughout Eastern Europe, Italy and France, is increasingly popular in Britain. The French are particularly enthusiastic: in autumn whole families drive to secret locations to comb the ground for prizes like shaggy ink caps or ceps. Wild mushrooms are sold in supermarkets.

OYSTER MUSHROOMS

These ear-shaped fungi grow on rotting wood. Cap, gills and stem are all the same colour, which can be greyish brown, pink or yellow. They are now widely cultivated, although they are generally thought of as wild mushrooms. Delicious both in flavour and texture, they are softer than the button mushroom when cooked but seem more substantial, having more "bite" to them.

Buying and Storing

Fresh specimens are erect and lively looking with clear gills and smooth caps. They are often sold packed in plastic

boxes under cellophane wrappings and will wilt and go soggy if left on the shelf for too long. Once purchased, remove them from the plastic packaging and use as soon as possible.

Preparing

Oyster mushrooms rarely need trimming at all but if they are large, tear rather than cut them into pieces. In very large specimens the stems can be tough and should be discarded.

Cooking

Fry in butter until tender – they take less time to cook than white mushrooms. Do not overcook oyster mushrooms as the flavour will be lost and the soft texture will become more rubbery.

Left: Pink and yellow oyster mushrooms.
Above: Grey oyster mushrooms.

ENOKITAKI MUSHROOMS

This is another Japanese mushroom. The wild variety is orangy-brown with shiny caps but outside Japan, you will probably only be able to find the cultivated variety, which are similarly fine, with pin-sized heads, but are pale coloured with snowy white caps. They have a fine, sweet and almost fruity flavour. In Japanese cookery they are added to salads or used as a garnish for soups or hot dishes. Since they become tough if overcooked, add enokitaki mushrooms at the very last minute of cooking.

SHIITAKE MUSHROOMS

These Japanese fungi are now commonly available in supermarkets. They are among a variety of tree mushrooms (called *take* in Japan, the *shii* being the hardwood tree from which they are harvested). They have a meaty, slightly acid flavour and a distinct slippery texture. Shiitake mushrooms, though once only available in oriental stores, are now widely available in most supermarkets. Unlike button mushrooms that can be flash-fried, shiitake need to be cooked through, although even this only takes 3-5 minutes. Add them to stir-fries for a delicious flavour and texture. Alternatively, fry them in oil until tender. Sprinkle with sesame oil and then serve with a little soy sauce.

Above: Enokitaki mushrooms.
Right: Shiitake mushrooms.

COOKING
WITH
VEGETABLES

CLASSIC FRENCH ONION SOUP

WHEN FRENCH ONION SOUP IS MADE SLOWLY AND CAREFULLY, THE ONIONS ALMOST CARAMELIZE TO A DEEP MAHOGANY COLOUR. IT HAS A SUPERB FLAVOUR AND IS A PERFECT WINTER SUPPER DISH.

SERVES FOUR

INGREDIENTS
   4 large onions
   30ml/2 tbsp sunflower or olive oil, or
      15ml/1 tbsp of each
   25g/1oz butter
   900ml/1½ pints/3¾ cups beef stock
   4 slices French bread
   40–50g/1½–2oz Gruyère or Cheddar
      cheese, grated
   salt and freshly ground black pepper

1 Peel and quarter the onions and slice or chop them into 5mm/¼in pieces. Heat the oil and butter together in a deep heavy-based saucepan, preferably with a medium-size base so that the onions form a thick layer.

3 When the onions are a rich mahogany brown, add the beef stock and a little seasoning. Simmer, partially covered, for 30 minutes, then taste and adjust the seasoning according to taste.

4 Preheat the grill and toast the French bread. Spoon the soup into four oven-proof serving dishes and place a piece of bread in each. Sprinkle with the cheese and grill for a few minutes until golden.

2 Fry the onions briskly for a few minutes, stirring constantly, and then reduce the heat and cook gently for 45–60 minutes. At first, the onions need to be stirred only occasionally but as they begin to colour, stir frequently. The colour of the onions gradually turns golden and then more rapidly to brown, so take care to stir constantly at this stage so they do not burn on the base.

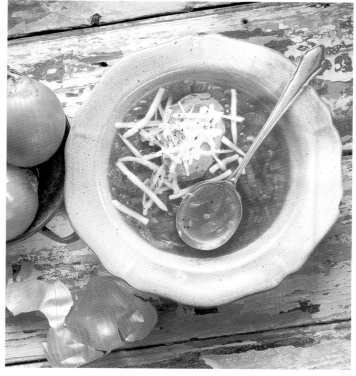

THAI NOODLES WITH CHINESE CHIVES

THIS RECIPE REQUIRES A LITTLE TIME FOR PREPARATION, BUT THE COOKING TIME IS VERY FAST. EVERYTHING IS COOKED SPEEDILY IN A HOT WOK AND SHOULD BE EATEN AT ONCE.

SERVES FOUR

INGREDIENTS

350g/12oz dried rice noodles
1cm/½ in fresh root ginger, grated
30ml/2 tbsp light soy sauce
45ml/3 tbsp vegetable oil
225g/8oz Quorn, cut into small cubes
2 garlic cloves, crushed
1 large onion, cut into thin wedges
115g/4oz fried bean curd, thinly sliced
1 green chilli, seeded
  and finely sliced
175g/6oz beansprouts
115g/4oz Chinese chives, cut into
  5cm/2in lengths
50g/2oz roasted peanuts, ground
30ml/2tbsp dark soy sauce
30ml/2 tbsp chopped fresh coriander
1 lemon, cut into wedges

1 Place the noodles in a large bowl, cover with warm water and soak for 20–30 minutes, then drain. Blend together the ginger, light soy sauce and 15ml/1 tbsp of the oil in a bowl. Stir in the Quorn and set aside for 10 minutes. Drain, reserving the marinade.

2 Heat 15ml/1 tbsp of the oil in a frying pan and fry the garlic for a few seconds. Add the Quorn and stir-fry for 3–4 minutes. Then transfer to a plate and set aside.

5 When hot, spoon on to serving plates and garnish with the remaining ground peanuts, coriander and lemon wedges.

COOK'S TIP
Quorn makes this a vegetarian meal, however thinly sliced pork or chicken could be used instead. Stir-fry it initially for 4–5 minutes.

3 Heat the remaining oil in the wok or frying pan and stir-fry the onion for 3–4 minutes until softened and tinged with brown. Add the bean curd and chilli, stir-fry briefly and then add the noodles. Stir-fry for 4–5 minutes.

4 Stir in the beansprouts, Chinese chives and most of the ground peanuts, reserving a little for the garnish. Stir well, then add the Quorn, the dark soy sauce and the reserved marinade.

LEEKS IN EGG AND LEMON SAUCE

THE COMBINATION OF EGGS AND LEMON IN SAUCES AND SOUPS IS COMMONLY FOUND IN RECIPES FROM GREECE, TURKEY AND THE MIDDLE EAST. THIS SAUCE HAS A DELICIOUS FRESH TASTE AND BRINGS OUT THE BEST IN THE LEEKS. BE SURE TO USE TENDER BABY LEEKS FOR THIS RECIPE.

SERVES FOUR

INGREDIENTS
675g/1½lb baby leeks
15ml/1 tbsp cornflour
10ml/2 tsp sugar
2 egg yolks
juice of 1½ lemons
salt

1 Trim the leeks, slit them from top to bottom and rinse very well under cold water to remove any dirt.

2 Place the leeks in a large saucepan, preferably so they lie flat on the base, cover with water and add a little salt. Bring to the boil, cover and simmer for 4–5 minutes until just tender.

3 Carefully remove the leeks using a slotted spoon, drain well and arrange in a shallow serving dish. Reserve 200ml/7fl oz/scant 1 cup of the cooking liquid.

4 Blend the cornflour with the cooled cooking liquid and place in a small saucepan. Bring to the boil, stirring all the time, and cook over a gentle heat until the sauce thickens slightly. Stir in the sugar and then remove the saucepan from the heat and allow to cool slightly.

5 Beat the egg yolks thoroughly with the lemon juice and stir gradually into the cooled sauce. Cook over a very low heat, stirring all the time, until the sauce is fairly thick. Be careful not to overheat the sauce or it may curdle. As soon as the sauce has thickened remove the pan from the heat and continue stirring for a minute. Taste and add salt or sugar as necessary. Cool slightly.

6 Stir the cooled sauce with a wooden spoon. Pour the sauce over the leeks and then cover and chill well for at least 2 hours before serving.

LEEK SOUFFLÉ

SOME PEOPLE THINK OF A SOUFFLÉ AS A DINNER PARTY DISH, AND A RATHER TRICKY ONE AT THAT. HOWEVER, OTHERS FREQUENTLY SERVE THEM FOR FAMILY MEALS BECAUSE THEY ARE QUICK AND EASY TO MAKE, AND PROVE TO BE VERY POPULAR AND SATISFYING.

SERVES TWO TO THREE

INGREDIENTS
    15ml/1 tbsp sunflower oil
    40g/1½oz butter
    2 leeks, thinly sliced
    about 300ml/½ pint/1¼ cups milk
    25g/1oz plain flour
    4 eggs, separated
    75g/3oz Gruyère or Emmenthal
        cheese, grated
    salt and freshly ground black pepper

1 Preheat the oven to 180°C/350°F Gas 4 and butter a large soufflé dish. Heat the oil and 15g/½oz of the butter in a small saucepan or flameproof casserole and fry the leeks over a gentle heat for 4–5 minutes until soft but not brown, stirring occasionally.

2 Stir in the milk and bring to the boil. Cover and simmer for 4–5 minutes until the leeks are tender. Strain the liquid through a sieve into a measuring jug.

3 Melt the remaining butter in a saucepan, stir in the flour and cook for 1 minute. Remove pan from the heat. Make up the reserved liquid with milk to 300ml/½ pint/1¼ cups. Gradually stir the milk into the pan to make a smooth sauce. Return to the heat and bring to the boil, stirring. When thickened, remove from the heat. Cool slightly and then beat in the egg yolks, cheese and the leeks.

4 Whisk the egg whites until stiff and, using a large metal spoon, fold into the leek and egg mixture. Pour into the prepared soufflé dish and bake in the oven for about 30 minutes until golden and puffy. Serve immediately.

TAGLIATELLE WITH LEEKS AND PARMA HAM

LEEKS ARE A VERY VERSATILE VEGETABLE. THEIR DELICATE, MILDLY ONIONY FLAVOUR MAKES THEM IDEAL TO USE IN STIR-FRIES, RISOTTOS, EGG DISHES, SOUPS AND SAUCES. IF USING OLDER LEEKS, MAKE SURE THEY HAVE NOT DEVELOPED A WOODY CORE.

SERVES FOUR

INGREDIENTS

5 leeks
40g/1½oz butter or margarine
225g/8oz tagliatelle, preferably
 green and white
20ml/4 tsp dry sherry
30ml/2 tbsp lemon juice
10ml/2 tsp chopped fresh basil
115–150g/4–5oz Parma ham,
 torn into strips
175g/6oz fromage frais
salt and freshly ground black pepper
fresh basil leaves, to garnish
Parmesan cheese, to serve

4 Stir the sherry, lemon juice, basil and seasoning into the leek mixture and cook for 1–2 minutes so that the flavours can blend together. Add the Parma ham and fromage frais, stir and cook for about 1–2 minutes until heated through.

5 Drain the pasta and place in a warmed serving dish. Pour the leek and Parma ham mixture on top and mix lightly together. Garnish each serving with basil leaves and serve with shavings of Parmesan cheese.

1 Trim the leeks and then cut a slit from top to bottom, rinse well under cold water and cut into thin slices.

2 Melt the butter or margarine in a saucepan or flameproof casserole, add the leeks and fry over a gentle heat for 3–4 minutes until tender but not too soft.

3 Add the tagliatelle to a large saucepan of boiling water and cook according to the instructions on the packet (about 3–5 minutes for fresh pasta; 8 minutes for dried pasta).

BAKED LEEKS <u>WITH</u> CHEESE <u>AND</u> YOGURT TOPPING

LIKE ALL VEGETABLES, THE FRESHER LEEKS ARE, THE BETTER THEIR FLAVOUR, AND THE FRESHEST LEEKS AVAILABLE SHOULD BE USED FOR THIS DISH. SMALL, YOUNG LEEKS ARE AROUND AT THE BEGINNING OF THE SEASON AND ARE PERFECT TO USE HERE.

SERVES FOUR

INGREDIENTS

8 small leeks, about 675g/1½lb
2 small eggs or 1 large one, beaten
150g/5oz fresh goat's cheese
85ml/3fl oz/⅓ cup natural yogurt
50g/2oz Parmesan cheese, grated
25g/1oz fresh white or brown
  breadcrumbs
salt and freshly ground black pepper

1 Preheat the oven to 180°C/350°F/Gas 4 and butter a shallow ovenproof dish. Trim the leeks, cut a slit from top to bottom and rinse well under cold water.

2 Place the leeks in a saucepan of water, bring to the boil and simmer gently for 6–8 minutes until just tender. Remove and drain well using a slotted spoon, and arrange in the prepared dish.

3 Beat the eggs with the goat's cheese, yogurt and half the Parmesan cheese, and season well with salt and pepper.

4 Pour the cheese and yogurt mixture over the leeks. Mix the breadcrumbs and remaining Parmesan cheese together and sprinkle over the sauce. Bake in the oven for 35–40 minutes until the top is crisp and golden brown.

CHICKEN WITH SHALLOTS

INGREDIENTS

1 small chicken, about 1.3kg/3lb,
  or 4 chicken pieces
seasoned plain flour, for coating
30ml/2 tbsp sunflower oil
25g/1oz butter
115g/4oz unsmoked streaky bacon,
  chopped
2 garlic cloves
450ml/¾ pint/1¾ cups red wine
1 bay leaf
2 thyme sprigs
250g/9oz shallots
115g/4oz button mushrooms,
  halved if large
10ml/2 tsp plain flour
salt and freshly ground black pepper

1 Preheat the oven to 180°C/350°F/
Gas 4. Remove any excess skin or fat
from the chicken and cut into four or
eight pieces. Place a little seasoned flour
in a large plastic bag, add the chicken
pieces and shake to coat evenly.

2 Heat half the oil and half the butter in
a large flameproof casserole and fry the
bacon and garlic for 3–4 minutes. Add
the chicken pieces and fry until lightly
browned. Add the wine, bay leaf and
thyme and bring to the boil. Cover and
cook in the oven for 1 hour.

3 Peel the shallots and boil them in
salted water for 10 minutes. Heat the
remaining oil in a small frying pan and
fry the shallots for 3–4 minutes until
beginning to brown. Add the mushrooms
and fry for a further 2–3 minutes.

4 Stir the shallots and mushrooms into
the casserole with the chicken and cook
for a further 8–10 minutes. Using a fork,
blend the flour with the remaining butter
to make a thick paste.

5 Transfer the chicken pieces, shallots
and mushrooms to a serving dish and
keep warm. Bring the liquid to the boil
and then add small pieces of the flour
paste, stirring vigorously after each
addition. When all the paste has been
added and the sauce is thick, either pour
over the chicken pieces or return the
chicken to the casserole and serve.

GLAZED SHALLOTS

INGREDIENTS

350–400g/12–14oz shallots
15ml/1 tbsp olive oil
25g/1oz butter
15ml/1 tbsp sugar
about 175ml/6fl oz/¾ cup water
salt and freshly ground black pepper

1 Peel the shallots and break in two if
the bulbs are joined. Heat the oil and
butter in a heavy-based saucepan and
gently fry the shallots over a moderate
heat for 5–6 minutes until patches of
brown begin to appear. Stir occasionally.

2 Sprinkle the shallots with the sugar
and cook, stirring, for 1 minute.

3 Add enough water to just cover the
shallots and then cover and simmer over
a low heat for about 25–35 minutes until
completely tender, adding a little extra
water if necessary, then remove the lid
and continue simmering gently until the
liquid has reduced to a thin syrup. Stir
occasionally. Season with salt, if liked.

4 Spoon the shallots into a serving dish
and pour over the syrup. Sprinkle with
black pepper. Serve with roast meat or a
baked vegetable dish.

ASPARAGUS SOUP

HOME-MADE ASPARAGUS SOUP HAS A DELICATE FLAVOUR, QUITE UNLIKE THAT FROM A CAN. THIS SOUP IS BEST MADE WITH YOUNG ASPARAGUS, WHICH IS TENDER AND BLENDS WELL. SERVE IT WITH WAFER-THIN SLICES OF BREAD.

SERVES FOUR

INGREDIENTS

450g/1lb young asparagus
40g/1½ oz butter
6 shallots, sliced
15g/½ oz plain flour
600ml/1 pint/2½ cups vegetable
   stock or water
15ml/1 tbsp lemon juice
250ml/8fl oz/1 cup milk
120ml/4fl oz/½ cup single cream
10ml/2 tsp chopped fresh chervil
salt and freshly ground black pepper

1 Trim the stalks of the asparagus if necessary. Cut 4cm/1½in off the tops of half the asparagus and set aside for a garnish. Slice the remaining asparagus.

2 Melt 25g/1oz of the butter in a large saucepan and gently fry the sliced shallots for 2–3 minutes until soft but not brown, stirring occasionally.

3 Add the sliced asparagus and fry over a gentle heat for about 1 minute. Stir in the flour and cook for 1 minute. Stir in the stock or water and lemon juice and season to taste. Bring to the boil and then simmer, partially covered, for 15–20 minutes until the asparagus is very tender.

4 Cool slightly and then process the soup in a food processor or blender until smooth. Then press the puréed asparagus through a sieve placed over a clean saucepan. Add the milk by pouring and stirring it through the sieve with the asparagus so as to extract the maximum amount of asparagus purée.

5 Melt the remaining butter and fry the reserved asparagus tips gently for about 3–4 minutes to soften.

6 Heat the soup gently for 3–4 minutes. Stir in the cream and the asparagus tips. Continue to heat gently and serve sprinkled with the chopped fresh chervil.

ROAST ASPARAGUS CRÊPES

ROAST ASPARAGUS IS DELICIOUS AND GOOD ENOUGH TO EAT JUST AS IT COMES. HOWEVER, FOR A REALLY SPLENDID STARTER, TRY THIS SIMPLE RECIPE. EITHER MAKE SIX LARGE OR TWICE AS MANY COCKTAIL-SIZE PANCAKES TO USE WITH SMALLER STEMS OF ASPARAGUS.

SERVES SIX

INGREDIENTS
90–120ml/6–8 tbsp olive oil
450g/1lb fresh asparagus
175g/6oz mascarpone cheese
60ml/4 tbsp single cream
25g/1oz Parmesan cheese, grated
sea salt
For the pancakes
175g/6oz plain flour
2 eggs
350ml/12fl oz/1½ cups milk
vegetable oil, for frying
pinch of salt

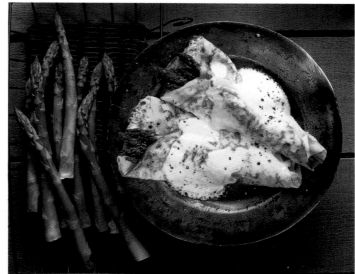

1 To make the pancake batter, mix the flour with the salt in a large bowl, food processor or blender, then add the eggs and milk and beat or process to make a smooth, fairly thin batter.

2 Heat a little oil in a large frying pan and add a small amount of batter, swirling the pan to coat the base evenly. Cook over a moderate heat for about 1 minute, then flip over and cook the other side until golden. Set aside and cook the rest of the pancakes in the same way; the mixture makes about six large or 12 smaller pancakes.

3 Preheat the oven to 180°C/350°F/Gas 4 and lightly grease a large shallow ovenproof dish or roasting tin with some of the olive oil.

4 Trim the asparagus by placing on a board and cutting off the bases. Using a small sharp knife, peel away the woody ends, if necessary.

5 Arrange the asparagus in a single layer in the dish, trickle over the remaining olive oil, rolling the asparagus to coat each one thoroughly. Sprinkle with a little salt and then roast in the oven for about 8–12 minutes until tender (the cooking time depends on the stem thickness).

6 Blend the mascarpone cheese with the cream and Parmesan cheese and spread a generous tablespoonful over each of the pancakes, leaving a little extra for the topping. Preheat the grill.

7 Divide the asparagus spears among the pancakes, roll up and arrange in a single layer in an ovenproof dish. Spoon over the remaining cheese mixture and then place under a moderate grill for 4–5 minutes, until heated through and golden brown. Serve at once.

ARTICHOKES WITH GARLIC AND HERB BUTTER

IT IS FUN EATING ARTICHOKES AND EVEN MORE FUN TO SHARE ONE BETWEEN TWO PEOPLE. YOU CAN ALWAYS HAVE A SECOND ONE TO FOLLOW SO THAT YOU GET YOUR FAIR SHARE!

SERVES FOUR

INGREDIENTS
    2 large or 4 medium globe artichokes
    salt
For the garlic and herb butter
    75g/3oz butter
    1 garlic clove, crushed
    15ml/1 tbsp mixed chopped fresh
        tarragon, marjoram and parsley

1 Wash the artichokes well in cold water. Using a sharp knife, cut off the stalks level with the bases. Cut off the top 1cm/½in of leaves. Snip off the pointed ends of the remaining leaves with scissors.

2 Put the prepared artichokes in a large saucepan of lightly salted water. Bring to the boil, cover and cook for about 40–45 minutes or until a lower leaf comes away easily when gently pulled.

3 Drain upside down for a couple of minutes while making the sauce. Melt the butter over a low heat, add the garlic and cook for 30 seconds. Remove from the heat, stir in the herbs and then pour into one or two small serving bowls.

4 Place the artichokes on serving plates and serve with the garlic and herb butter.

COOK'S TIP
To eat an artichoke, pull off each leaf and dip into the garlic and herb butter. Scrape off the soft fleshy base with your teeth. When the centre is reached, pull out the hairy choke and discard it, as it is inedible. The base can be cut up and eaten with the remaining garlic butter.

STUFFED ARTICHOKES

THE AMOUNT OF STUFFING NEEDED FOR THIS DISH DEPENDS ON THE SIZE OF THE ARTICHOKES — IF THEY ARE SMALL YOU COULD SERVE ONE PER PERSON. TO INCREASE THE AMOUNT OF STUFFING, ADD EXTRA MOZZARELLA AND LEEK RATHER THAN BACON.

SERVES FOUR (as a starter)

INGREDIENTS
   2 globe artichokes, prepared
   lemon juice
For the stuffing
   25g/1oz butter
   2–3 small leeks, sliced
   2–3 bacon rashers, chopped (optional)
   75g/3oz mozzarella cheese, cut into
     small cubes
   25–40g/1–1½oz fresh brown or white
     breadcrumbs
   5ml/1 tsp chopped fresh basil
   fresh basil leaves, to garnish
   salt and freshly ground black pepper

1 Place the artichokes in a large saucepan of salted water. Bring to the boil, cover and cook for 35–40 minutes or until a lower leaf comes away easily.

3 Drain the artichokes, upside-down, and when cool enough to handle, cut in half from top to bottom using a sharp knife. Remove the inner leaves, pull out and discard the choke and then sprinkle the inside and base liberally with lemon juice to prevent discolouration.

4 Preheat the grill. Spoon a little of the stuffing into each artichoke half and place them in a single layer in an oven-proof dish. Set under a moderately hot grill and grill for 5–6 minutes until the stuffing is golden brown. Serve on small plates garnished with basil leaves.

2 To make the stuffing, melt the butter in a saucepan and gently fry the leeks for 3–4 minutes. Add the bacon, if using, and continue frying until the leek is soft and the bacon lightly golden brown. Remove the pan from the heat and stir in the mozzarella cubes, breadcrumbs, basil and seasoning to taste.

CELERIAC GRATIN

ALTHOUGH CELERIAC HAS A RATHER UNATTRACTIVE APPEARANCE WITH ITS HARD, KNOBBLY SKIN, IT IS A VEGETABLE THAT HAS A VERY DELICIOUS SWEET AND NUTTY FLAVOUR. THIS IS ACCENTUATED IN THIS DISH BY THE ADDITION OF THE SWEET YET NUTTY EMMENTAL CHEESE.

SERVES FOUR

INGREDIENTS
  450g/1lb celeriac
  juice of ½ lemon
  25g/1oz butter
  1 small onion, finely chopped
  30ml/2 tbsp plain flour
  300ml/½ pint/1¼ cups milk
  25g/1oz Emmental cheese, grated
  15ml/1 tbsp capers
  salt and cayenne pepper

1 Preheat the oven to 190°C/375°F/ Gas 5. Peel the celeriac and cut into 5mm/¼in slices, immediately plunging them into a saucepan of cold water acidulated with the lemon juice.

2 Bring the water to the boil and simmer the celeriac for 10–12 minutes until just tender. Drain and arrange the celeriac in a shallow ovenproof dish.

3 Melt the butter in a small saucepan and fry the onion over a gentle heat until soft but not browned. Stir in the flour, cook for 1 minute and then slowly stir in the milk to make a smooth sauce. Stir in the cheese, capers and seasoning to taste and then pour over the celeriac. Cook in the oven for 15–20 minutes until the top is golden brown.

VARIATION
For a less strongly flavoured dish, alternate the layers of celeriac with potato. Slice the potato, cook until almost tender, then drain well before assembling the dish.

CELERIAC AND BLUE CHEESE ROULADE

CELERIAC ADDS A DELICATE AND SUBTLE FLAVOUR TO THIS ATTRACTIVE DISH. THE SPINACH ROULADE
MAKES AN ATTRACTIVE CONTRAST TO THE CREAMY FILLING BUT YOU COULD USE A PLAIN OR CHEESE
ROULADE BASE INSTEAD. BE SURE TO ROLL UP THE ROULADE WHILE IT IS STILL WARM AND PLIABLE.

SERVES SIX

INGREDIENTS
   15g/½oz butter
   225g/8oz cooked spinach, drained
     and chopped
   150ml/¼ pint/⅔ cup single cream
   4 large eggs, separated
   15g/½oz Parmesan cheese, grated
   pinch of nutmeg
   salt and freshly ground black pepper
For the filling
   225g/8oz celeriac
   lemon juice
   75g/3oz St Agur cheese
   115g/4oz fromage frais
   freshly ground black pepper

1 Preheat the oven to 200°C/400°F/
Gas 6 and line a 34 x 24cm/13 x 9in Swiss
roll tin with non-stick baking paper.

2 Melt the butter in a saucepan and add
the spinach. Cook gently until all the
liquid has evaporated, stirring frequently.
Remove the pan from the heat and stir in
the cream, egg yolks, Parmesan cheese,
nutmeg and seasoning.

4 Bake in the oven for 10–15 minutes
until the roulade is firm to the touch and
lightly golden on top. Carefully turn out
on to a sheet of greaseproof or non-stick
baking paper and peel away the lining
paper. Roll it up with the paper inside
and leave to cool slightly.

5 To make the filling, peel and grate the
celeriac into a bowl and sprinkle well
with lemon juice. Blend the blue cheese
and fromage frais together and mix with
the celeriac and a little black pepper.

6 Unroll the roulade, spread with the
filling and roll up again. Serve at once or
wrap loosely and chill.

3 Whisk the egg whites until stiff, fold
them gently into the spinach mixture and
then spoon into the prepared tin. Spread
the mixture evenly and use a palette
knife to smooth the surface.

Spring Rolls

Bamboo shoots and beansprouts are perfect companions in this popular snack, providing the contrast in texture that is the principal element in Chinese cooking. The bamboo shoots retain their crispness, while the beansprouts become more chewy when cooked.

MAKES ABOUT TWENTY

INGREDIENTS
  60ml/4 tbsp vegetable oil
  30ml/2 tbsp dark soy sauce
  30ml/2 tbsp medium dry sherry
  about 1cm/½in fresh root ginger,
    finely grated
  225g/8oz minced Quorn
  50g/2oz rice vermicelli
  4–5 shiitake mushrooms
  4–5 spring onions
  200g/7oz can bamboo shoots
  1 garlic clove, crushed
  1 carrot, grated
  75g/3oz beansprouts, roughly
    chopped
  15ml/1 tbsp cornflour, blended
    with 30ml/2 tbsp water
  about 20 15cm/6in spring roll
    wrappers
  vegetable oil, for deep frying

1 Blend together 30ml/2 tbsp of the oil, the soy sauce, sherry and ginger in a medium-size bowl. Add the Quorn, stir well and set aside for 10–15 minutes.

2 Place the rice vermicelli in a large bowl, cover with boiling water and leave to stand for 15–20 minutes. Drain well and then chop roughly.

3 Wipe the mushrooms, remove the stalks and slice the caps thinly, halving them if the mushrooms are large.

4 Using a sharp knife, cut the spring onions into diagonal slices, including all but the tips of the green parts.

5 Drain the bamboo shoots and rinse them very well under cold running water. Cut in half if they are large.

6 Heat 15ml/1 tbsp of the remaining oil in a wok or large frying pan and cook the garlic for a few seconds. Add the spring onions and stir-fry for 2–3 minutes. Add the mushrooms and stir-fry for a further 3–4 minutes. Transfer the vegetables to a plate, using a slotted spoon.

7 Heat the remaining oil in the wok. Drain the Quorn, reserving the marinade, and then stir-fry for 4–5 minutes.

8 Add the bamboo shoots to the Quorn together with the carrot, vermicelli, the mushroom and onion mixture and the reserved marinade, and stir well. Add the beansprouts, stir well and then remove from the heat and cool.

9 Place a level tablespoon of mixture at one corner of a spring roll sheet. Brush the edges of the pastry with the cornflour mixture and roll up, folding the left and right corners inwards as you roll. Continue making spring rolls in this way, until all the mixture is used up.

10 Heat some oil in a large wok or deep-fryer and fry two or three rolls at a time for 3–4 minutes until golden, turning them so that they cook evenly. Drain on kitchen paper and keep warm. Serve with extra soy sauce.

SAMPHIRE WITH CHILLED FISH CURRY

EVEN IF YOU'RE A BIG CURRY FAN, DON'T BE TEMPTED TO ADD TOO MUCH CURRY PASTE TO THIS DISH.
YOU NEED ONLY THE MEREST HINT OF MILD CURRY PASTE SO THAT THE FLAVOUR OF THE SAMPHIRE AND
FISH CAN STILL BE APPRECIATED.

SERVES FOUR

INGREDIENTS
175g/6oz samphire
350g/12oz fresh salmon steak or fillet
350g/12oz lemon sole fillets
fish stock or water
115g/4oz large peeled prawns
25g/1oz butter
1 small onion, very finely chopped
10ml/2 tsp mild curry paste
5–10ml/1–2 tsp apricot jam
150ml/¼ pint/⅔ cup soured cream
sprig of mint, to garnish (optional)

1 Trim the samphire and blanch in boiling water for about 5 minutes until tender. Drain and set aside.

2 Place the salmon and lemon sole in a large frying pan, cover with fish stock or water and bring to the boil. Reduce the heat, cover and cook for 6–8 minutes until the fish is tender.

COOK'S TIP
As the samphire has a fresh salty tang of the sea, there is not really any need to add extra salt to this recipe.

3 Transfer the fish to a plate and when cool enough to handle, break the salmon and sole into bite-size pieces, removing any skin and bones. Place in a mixing bowl with the prawns.

4 Melt the butter in a saucepan and gently fry the onion for 3–4 minutes until soft but not brown. Add the curry paste, cook for 30 seconds, then remove from the heat. Stir in the jam. Allow to cool and then stir in the soured cream.

5 Pour the curry cream over the fish. Arrange the samphire around the edge of a serving plate and spoon the fish into the centre. Garnish with a sprig of mint.

FENNEL AND MUSSEL PROVENÇAL

SERVES FOUR

INGREDIENTS
2 large fennel bulbs
1.75kg/4–4½lb fresh mussels in
  their shells, well scrubbed under
  cold water and beards removed
175ml/6fl oz/¾ cup water
sprig of thyme
25g/1oz butter
4 shallots, finely chopped
1 garlic clove, crushed
250ml/8fl oz/1 cup white wine
10ml/2 tsp plain flour
175ml/6fl oz/¾ cup single cream
15ml/1 tbsp chopped fresh parsley
salt and freshly ground black pepper
sprig of dill, to garnish

1 Trim the fennel, cut into slices
5mm/¼in thick and then cut into
1cm/½in sticks. Cook in a little salted
water until just tender and drain.

2 Discard any mussels that are
damaged or do not close. Put in a large
saucepan, add the water and thyme,
cover tightly, bring to the boil and cook
for about 5 minutes until the mussels
open, shaking occasionally.

3 Transfer the mussels to a plate and
discard any that are unopened. When
cool enough to handle, remove them
from their shells, reserving a few in their
shells for a garnish.

4 Melt the butter in a saucepan and fry
the shallots and garlic for 3–4 minutes
until softened but not browned. Add the
fennel, fry briefly for 30–60 seconds and
then stir in the wine and simmer gently
until the liquid is reduced by half.

5 Blend the flour with a little extra wine
or water. Add the cream, parsley and
seasoning to the saucepan and heat
gently. Stir in the blended flour and the
mussels. Cook over a low heat until the
sauce thickens. Season to taste and pour
into a warmed serving dish. Garnish with
dill and reserved mussels in their shells.

BRAISED FENNEL WITH TOMATOES

SERVES FOUR

INGREDIENTS
3 small fennel bulbs
30–45ml/2–3 tbsp olive oil
5–6 shallots, sliced
2 garlic cloves, crushed
4 tomatoes, peeled and chopped
about 175ml/6fl oz/¾ cup dry
  white wine
15ml/1 tbsp chopped fresh basil or
  2.5ml/½ tsp dried
40–50g/1½–2oz fresh white breadcrumbs
salt and freshly ground black pepper

1 Preheat the oven to 150°C/300°F/
Gas 2. Trim the fennel bulbs and cut into
slices about 1cm/½ in thick.

2 Heat the olive oil in a large saucepan
and fry the shallots and garlic for about
4–5 minutes over a moderate heat until
the shallots are slightly softened. Add the
tomatoes, stir-fry briefly and then stir in
150ml/¼ pint/⅔ cup of the wine, the basil
and seasoning. Bring to the boil, add the
fennel, then cover and cook for 5 minutes.

3 Arrange the fennel in layers in an
ovenproof dish. Pour over the tomato
mixture and sprinkle the top with half the
breadcrumbs. Bake in the oven for about
1 hour. From time to time, press down on
the breadcrumb crust with the back of a
spoon and sprinkle over another layer of
breadcrumbs and a little more of the
wine. The crust slowly becomes golden
brown and very crunchy.

HASSELBACK POTATOES

A VERY UNUSUAL WAY WITH POTATOES. EACH POTATO HALF IS SLICED ALMOST TO THE BASE AND THEN ROASTED WITH OIL AND BUTTER. THE CRISPY POTATOES ARE THEN COATED IN AN ORANGE GLAZE AND RETURNED TO THE OVEN UNTIL DEEP GOLDEN BROWN AND CRUNCHY.

SERVES FOUR TO SIX

INGREDIENTS
    4 large potatoes
    25g/1oz butter, melted
    45ml/3 tbsp olive oil
For the glaze
    juice of 1 orange
    grated rind of ½ orange
    15ml/1 tbsp demerara sugar
    freshly ground black pepper

1 Preheat the oven to 190°C/375°F/Gas 5. Cut each potato in half length-ways, place flat-side down and then cut down as if making very thin slices, but leaving the bottom 1cm/½in intact.

2 Place the potatoes in a large roasting dish. Using a pastry brush, coat the potatoes generously with the melted butter and pour the olive oil over the base and around the potatoes.

3 Bake the potatoes in the oven for 40–50 minutes until they begin to brown. Baste occasionally during cooking.

4 Meanwhile, place the orange juice, orange rind and sugar in a small saucepan and heat gently, stirring until the sugar has dissolved. Simmer for 3–4 minutes until the glaze is fairly thick and then remove from the heat.

5 When the potatoes begin to brown, brush all over with the orange glaze and return to the oven to roast for a further 15 minutes or until the potatoes are a deep golden brown. Serve at once.

PUFFY CREAMED POTATOES

THIS ACCOMPANIMENT CONSISTS OF CREAMED POTATOES INCORPORATED INTO MINI YORKSHIRE PUDDINGS. SERVE THEM WITH ROAST DUCK OR BEEF, OR WITH A VEGETARIAN CASSEROLE. FOR A MEAL ON ITS OWN, SERVE TWO OR THREE PER PERSON AND ACCOMPANY WITH SALADS.

MAKES SIX

INGREDIENTS
    275g/10oz potatoes
    creamy milk and butter for mashing
    5ml/1 tsp chopped fresh parsley
    5ml/1 tsp chopped fresh tarragon
    75g/3oz plain flour
    1 egg
    about 120ml/4fl oz/½ cup milk
    oil or sunflower fat, for baking
    salt and freshly ground black pepper

1 Boil the potatoes until tender and mash with a little milk and butter. Stir in the chopped parsley and tarragon and season well to taste. Preheat the oven to 200°C/400°F/Gas 6.

2 Process the flour, egg, milk and a little salt in a food processor or blender to make a smooth batter.

3 Place about 2.5ml/½ tsp oil or a small knob of sunflower fat in each of six ramekin dishes and place in the oven on a baking tray for 2–3 minutes until the oil or fat is very hot.

4 Working quickly, pour a small amount of batter (about 20ml/4 tsp) into each ramekin dish. Add a heaped tablespoon of mashed potatoes and then pour an equal amount of the remaining batter in each dish. Place in the oven and bake for 15–20 minutes until the puddings are puffy and golden brown.

5 Using a palette knife, carefully ease the puddings out of the ramekin dishes and arrange on a large warm serving dish. Serve at once.

PARSNIP AND CHESTNUT CROQUETTES

THE SWEET NUTTY TASTE OF CHESTNUTS BLENDS PERFECTLY WITH THE SIMILARLY SWEET BUT EARTHY FLAVOUR OF PARSNIPS. FRESH CHESTNUTS NEED TO BE PEELED BUT FROZEN CHESTNUTS ARE EASY TO USE AND ARE NEARLY AS GOOD AS FRESH FOR THIS RECIPE.

MAKES TEN TO TWELVE

INGREDIENTS

450g/1lb parsnips, cut roughly into
   small pieces
115g/4oz frozen chestnuts
25g/1oz butter
1 garlic clove, crushed
15ml/1tbsp chopped fresh coriander
1 egg, beaten
40–50g/1½–2oz fresh white
   breadcrumbs
vegetable oil, for frying
salt and freshly ground black pepper
sprig of coriander, to garnish

1 Place the parsnips in a saucepan with enough water to cover. Bring to the boil, cover and simmer for 15–20 minutes until completely tender.

2 Place the frozen chestnuts in a pan of water, bring to the boil and simmer for 8–10 minutes until very tender. Drain, place in a bowl and mash roughly.

3 Melt the butter in a small saucepan and cook the garlic for 30 seconds. Drain the parsnips and mash with the garlic butter. Stir in the chestnuts and chopped coriander, then season well.

4 Take about 15ml/1tbsp of the mixture at a time and form into small croquettes, about 7.5cm/3in long. Dip each croquette into the beaten egg and then roll in the breadcrumbs.

5 Heat a little oil in a frying pan and fry the croquettes for 3–4 minutes until golden, turning frequently so they brown evenly. Drain on kitchen paper and then serve at once, garnished with coriander.

PARSNIP, AUBERGINE AND CASHEW BIRYANI

SERVES FOUR TO SIX

INGREDIENTS
1 small aubergine, sliced
275g/10oz basmati rice
3 parsnips
3 onions
2 garlic cloves
2.5cm/1in piece fresh root ginger,
  peeled
about 60ml/4 tbsp vegetable oil
175g/6oz unsalted cashew nuts
40g/1½oz sultanas
1 red pepper, seeded and sliced
5ml/1 tsp ground cumin
5ml/1 tsp ground coriander
2.5ml/½ tsp chilli powder
120ml/4fl oz/½ cup natural yogurt
300ml/½ pint/1¼ cups vegetable
  or chicken stock
25g/1oz butter
salt and freshly ground black pepper
sprigs of coriander, to garnish
2 hard-boiled eggs, quartered

1 Sprinkle the aubergine with salt and leave for 30 minutes. Rinse, pat dry and cut into bite-size pieces. Soak the rice in a bowl of cold water for 40 minutes. Peel and core the parsnips. Cut into 1cm/½in pieces. Roughly chop 1 onion and put in a food processor or blender with the garlic and ginger. Add 30–45ml/2–3 tbsp water and process to a paste.

2 Finely slice the remaining onions. Heat 45ml/3 tbsp of the oil in a large flameproof casserole and fry gently for 10–15 minutes until deep golden brown. Remove and drain. Add 40g/1½oz of the cashew nuts to the pan and stir-fry for 2 minutes. Add the sultanas and fry until they swell. Remove and drain.

3 Add the aubergine and pepper to the pan and stir-fry for 4–5 minutes. Drain on kitchen paper. Fry the parsnips for 4–5 minutes. Stir in the remaining cashew nuts and fry for 1 minute. Transfer to the plate with the aubergines.

4 Add the remaining 15ml/1 tbsp of oil to the pan. Add the onion paste. Cook, stirring over a moderate heat for 4–5 minutes until the mixture turns golden. Stir in the cumin, coriander and chilli powder. Cook, stirring, for 1 minute, then reduce the heat and add the yogurt.

5 Bring the mixture slowly to the boil and stir in the stock, parsnips, aubergines and peppers. Season, cover and simmer for 30–40 minutes until the parsnips are tender and then transfer to an ovenproof casserole.

6 Preheat the oven to 150°C/300°F/ Gas 2. Drain the rice and add to 300ml/ ½ pint/1¼ cups of salted boiling water. Cook gently for 5–6 minutes until it is tender but slightly undercooked.

7 Drain the rice and pile it in a mound on top of the parsnips. Make a hole from the top to the base using the handle of a wooden spoon. Scatter the reserved fried onions, cashew nuts and sultanas over the rice and dot with butter. Cover with a double layer of foil and then secure in place with a lid.

8 Cook in the oven for 35–40 minutes. To serve, spoon the mixture on to a warmed serving dish and garnish with coriander sprigs and quartered eggs.

CARROT AND CORIANDER SOUP

NEARLY ALL ROOT VEGETABLES MAKE EXCELLENT SOUPS AS THEY PURÉE WELL AND HAVE AN EARTHY FLAVOUR WHICH COMPLEMENTS THE SHARPER FLAVOURS OF HERBS AND SPICES. CARROTS ARE PARTICULARLY VERSATILE AND THIS SIMPLE SOUP IS ELEGANT IN BOTH FLAVOUR AND APPEARANCE.

SERVES FOUR TO SIX

INGREDIENTS
   450g/1lb carrots, preferably young
      and tender
   15ml/1 tbsp sunflower oil
   40g/1½oz butter
   1 onion, chopped
   1 celery stalk, sliced plus 2–3 pale
      leafy celery tops
   2 small potatoes, chopped
   1 litre/1¾ pints/4 cups chicken stock
   10–15ml/2–3 tsp ground coriander
   15ml/1 tbsp chopped fresh coriander
   200ml/7fl oz/⅞ cup milk
   salt and freshly ground black pepper

1 Trim the carrots, peel if necessary and cut into chunks. Heat the oil and 25g/1oz of the butter in a large flame-proof casserole or heavy-based saucepan and fry the onion over a gentle heat for 3–4 minutes until slightly softened but not browned.

2 Cut the celery stalk into slices. Add the celery and potatoes to the onion in the pan, cook for a few minutes and then add the carrots. Fry over a gentle heat for 3–4 minutes, stirring frequently, and then cover. Reduce the heat even further and sweat for about 10 minutes. Shake the pan or stir occasionally so the vegetables do not stick to the base.

3 Add the stock, bring to the boil and then partially cover and simmer for a further 8–10 minutes until the carrots and potatoes are tender.

4 Remove 6–8 tiny celery leaves for garnish and finely chop the remaining celery tops (about 15ml/1 tbsp once chopped). Melt the remaining butter in a small saucepan and fry the ground coriander for about 1 minute, stirring constantly.

5 Reduce the heat and add the chopped celery and fresh coriander and fry for about 1 minute. Set aside.

6 Process the soup in a food processor or blender and pour into a clean saucepan. Stir in the milk, coriander mixture and seasoning. Heat gently, taste and adjust the seasoning. Serve garnished with the reserved celery.

COOK'S TIP
For a more piquant flavour, add a little lemon juice just before serving.

BORSCHT

THIS CLASSIC SOUP WAS THE STAPLE DIET OF PRE-REVOLUTION RUSSIAN PEASANTS FOR HUNDREDS OF YEARS. THERE ARE MANY VARIATIONS AND IT IS RARE TO FIND TWO RECIPES THE SAME.

SERVES SIX

INGREDIENTS

    350g/12oz whole, uncooked beetroot
    15ml/1 tbsp sunflower oil
    115g/4oz streaky bacon, chopped
    1 large onion
    1 large carrot, cut into julienne strips
    3 celery stalks, thinly sliced
    1.5 litres/2½ pints/6¼ cups chicken
      stock
    about 225g/8oz tomatoes, peeled,
      seeded and sliced
    about 30ml/2 tbsp lemon juice
      or wine vinegar
    30ml/2 tbsp chopped dill
    115g/4oz white cabbage, thinly sliced
    150ml/¼ pint/⅔ cup soured cream
    salt and freshly ground black pepper

1 Peel the beetroot, slice and then cut into very thin strips.

2 Heat the oil in a large, heavy-based saucepan and fry the bacon over a gentle heat for 3–4 minutes. Add the onion, fry for 2–3 minutes and then add the carrot, celery and beetroot. Cook for 4–5 minutes, stirring frequently, until the oil has been absorbed.

3 Add the stock, tomatoes, lemon juice or wine vinegar, half of the dill and seasoning. Bring to the boil and simmer for about 30–40 minutes until the vegetables are completely tender.

4 Add the cabbage and simmer for 5 minutes until tender. Adjust the seasoning and serve sprinkled with remaining dill and the soured cream.

POUSSINS WITH SWEET POTATO CHIPS

SERVES FOUR

INGREDIENTS
    4 poussins, about 275–350g/
      10–12oz each
    175–250ml/6–8fl oz/¾–1 cup chicken
      stock
    175ml/6fl oz/¾ cup white wine
    30ml/2 tbsp lemon juice
    15ml/1 tbsp chopped fresh tarragon or
      10ml/2 tsp dried
    25g/1oz butter
    10ml/2 tsp plain flour
    salt and freshly ground black pepper
For the stuffing
    1 sweet potato, about 225g/8oz
    15ml/1 tbsp lemon juice
    25g/1oz butter or margarine
    2 shallots, finely chopped
    25g/1oz flaked almonds
    50g/2oz ready-to-eat apricots,
      chopped
    25g/1oz fresh brown or white
      breadcrumbs
    5ml/1 tsp chopped fresh thyme
    salt and freshly ground black pepper
For the sweet potato chips
    450g/1lb sweet potatoes
    juice of ½ lemon
    flour, for coating
    good pinch of cayenne pepper
    good pinch of ground coriander
    good pinch of ground cumin
    oil, for deep frying

1 Preheat the oven to 180°C/350°F/
Gas 4 and prepare the stuffing. Peel the
sweet potato and cook in boiling water
with the lemon juice until tender. Drain
and mash with half of the butter.

2 Melt the remaining butter in a small
frying pan and fry the shallots for 2–3
minutes until softened. Add the almonds
and continue frying until both the
almonds and shallots are flecked with
brown. Stir into the mashed potato
together with the apricots, breadcrumbs,
thyme and seasoning to taste.

3 Loosely stuff the poussins with the
mixture and place them in a roasting tin.
Mix together the stock, white wine and
lemon juice in a small saucepan and
bring to the boil. Pour over the poussins.

4 Sprinkle each with tarragon and
seasoning and use half the butter to dot
evenly over each bird.

5 Cover loosely with foil and roast in the
oven for 35–45 minutes, basting often
with the juices.

6 To prepare the sweet potato chips,
peel and thinly slice the potatoes and
place in a bowl of water with the lemon
juice. Mix the flour, cayenne pepper,
ground coriander, ground cumin and
some salt on a plate.

7 Ten minutes before the poussins are
ready, heat the oil in a deep fryer or wok.
Drain, then dry the potato slices with
kitchen paper and dip into the seasoned
flour. Fry the slices, in batches, for 2–3
minutes until golden. Drain well on
kitchen paper and keep warm.

8 When the poussins are cooked and
the juices run clear, increase the oven
temperature to 220°C/425°F/Gas 7. Cook
uncovered for 5 minutes or until well
browned. Transfer to a serving plate and
arrange the sweet potato chips around
the edge.

9 Pour the cooking juices into a
saucepan and heat gently. Mix the
remaining butter and flour to a paste and
add small pieces to the stock, whisking
well between each addition. Pour the
sauce into a jug and serve with the
poussins and potato chips.

CASSAVA AND VEGETABLE KEBABS

This is an attractive and delicious assortment of African vegetables, marinated in a spicy garlic sauce. If cassava is unavailable, use sweet potato or yam instead.

SERVES FOUR

INGREDIENTS

175g/6oz cassava
1 onion, cut into wedges
1 aubergine, cut into bite-size pieces
1 courgette, sliced
1 ripe plantain, sliced
1 red pepper or ½ red pepper, ½ green pepper, sliced
16 cherry tomatoes
For the marinade
60ml/4 tbsp lemon juice
60ml/4 tbsp olive oil
45–60/3–4 tbsp soy sauce
15ml/1 tbsp tomato purée
1 green chilli, seeded and finely chopped
½ onion, grated
2 garlic cloves, crushed
5ml/1 tsp mixed spice
pinch of dried thyme
rice or couscous, to serve

1 Peel the cassava and cut into bite-size pieces. Place in a bowl, cover with boiling water and leave to blanch for 5 minutes. Drain well.

2 Place all the vegetables, including the cassava, in a large bowl.

3 Blend together all the marinade ingredients and pour over the prepared vegetables. Set aside for 1–2 hours.

4 Preheat the grill and thread all the vegetables and cherry tomatoes on to eight skewers.

5 Grill the vegetables under a low heat for about 15 minutes until tender and browned, turning frequently and basting occasionally with the marinade.

6 Meanwhile, pour the remaining marinade into a small saucepan and simmer for 10 minutes until slightly reduced.

7 Arrange the vegetable kebabs on a serving plate and strain the sauce into a small jug. Serve with rice or couscous.

PAN-FRIED SWEET POTATOES <u>WITH</u> BACON

THIS IS A COMFORTING DISH TO EAT ON A COLD WINTER'S EVENING. BACON AND ONION COUNTERACT THE SWEETNESS OF THE POTATO, AND THE CAYENNE PEPPER GIVES THE NECESSARY EXTRA "BITE".

SERVES FOUR

INGREDIENTS

675–900g/1½–2lb sweet potatoes
juice of 1 lemon
15ml/1 tbsp plain flour
a good pinch of cayenne pepper
about 45ml/3 tbsp sunflower oil
1 large onion, chopped
115g/4oz streaky bacon, chopped
50g/2oz fresh brown or white
   breadcrumbs
salt

1 Peel the sweet potatoes and cut into chunks about 4cm/1½in square. Place in a pan of boiling water with the lemon juice and a little salt and simmer for 8–10 minutes until cooked but not soft.

2 Mix together the flour, cayenne pepper and a pinch of salt. Drain the potatoes and then dust with the seasoned flour, coating the pieces well.

3 Heat 15ml/1tbsp of the oil in a large frying pan and fry the onion for about 2 minutes. Add the bacon and fry over a gentle heat for 6–8 minutes until the onion and bacon are golden. Transfer to a plate using a slotted spoon.

4 Add the breadcrumbs and fry, stirring, for about 1–2 minutes until golden. Add to the plate with the bacon.

5 Heat the remaining oil in the pan and fry the potatoes for 5–6 minutes, turning occasionally, until evenly browned. Stir in the breadcrumb and bacon mixture and cook for 1 minute. Serve at once.

SALSIFY GRATIN

THE SPINACH IN THIS RECIPE ADDS COLOUR AND MAKES IT GO FURTHER. HOWEVER, IF YOU CAN OBTAIN SALSIFY EASILY AND HAVE THE PATIENCE TO PEEL A LOT OF IT, INCREASE THE QUANTITY AND LEAVE OUT THE SPINACH. FOR VEGETARIANS USE VEGETABLE INSTEAD OF CHICKEN STOCK.

SERVES FOUR

INGREDIENTS
   450g/1lb salsify, cut into
     5cm/2in lengths
   juice of 1½ lemons
   450g/1lb spinach, prepared
   150ml/¼ pint/⅔ cup chicken stock
   300ml/½ pint/1¼ cups single cream
   salt and freshly ground black pepper

3 Cook the spinach in a large saucepan over a moderate heat for 2–3 minutes until the leaves have wilted, shaking the pan occasionally. Place the stock, cream and seasoning in a small saucepan and heat through very gently, stirring.

4 Arrange the salsify and spinach in layers in the prepared dish. Pour over the stock and cream mixture and bake in the oven for about 1 hour until the top is golden brown and bubbling.

1 Trim away the tops and bottoms of the salsify and peel or scrape away the outer skin. Place each peeled root immediately in water with lemon juice added, to prevent discolouration.

2 Preheat the oven to 160°C/325°F/ Gas 3 and butter an ovenproof dish. Place the salsify in a saucepan of boiling water with the lemon juice. Simmer for about 10 minutes until the salsify is just tender, then drain.

SPINACH AND CANNELLINI BEANS

THIS HEARTY DISH CAN BE MADE WITH ALMOST ANY DRIED BEAN, SUCH AS BLACK-EYED BEANS, HARICOTS OR CHICK-PEAS. IT IS A GOOD DISH TO SERVE ON A COLD EVENING. IF USING CANNED BEANS, DRAIN, THEN RINSE UNDER COLD WATER.

SERVES FOUR

INGREDIENTS
225g/8oz cannellini beans,
  soaked overnight
60ml/4 tbsp olive oil
1 slice white bread
1 onion, chopped
3–4 tomatoes, peeled and chopped
a good pinch of paprika
450g/1lb spinach
1 garlic clove, halved
salt and freshly ground black pepper

1 Drain the beans, place in a saucepan and cover with water. Bring to the boil and boil rapidly for 10 minutes. Cover and simmer for about 1 hour until the beans are tender. Drain.

2 Heat 30ml/2 tbsp of the oil in a frying pan and fry the bread until golden brown. Transfer to a plate.

3 Fry the onion in 15ml/1 tbsp of the oil over a gentle heat until soft but not brown, then add the tomatoes and continue cooking over a gentle heat.

4 Heat the remaining oil in a large pan, stir in the paprika and then add the spinach. Cover and cook for a few minutes until the spinach has wilted.

5 Add the onion and tomato mixture to the spinach, mix well and stir in the cannellini beans. Place the garlic and fried bread in a food processor and process until smooth. Stir into the spinach and bean mixture. Add 150ml/¼ pint/⅔ cup cold water and then cover and simmer gently for 20–30 minutes, adding more water if necessary.

SPINACH IN FILO WITH THREE CHEESES

A GOOD CHOICE TO SERVE WHEN VEGETARIANS AND MEAT EATERS ARE GATHERED FOR A MEAL AS, WHATEVER THEIR PREFERENCE, EVERYONE SEEMS PARTIAL TO THIS TASTY DISH.

SERVES FOUR

INGREDIENTS
450g/1lb spinach
15ml/1 tbsp sunflower oil
15g/½oz butter
1 small onion, finely chopped
175g/6oz ricotta cheese
115g/4oz feta cheese, cut into
  small cubes
75g/3oz Gruyère or Emmenthal
  cheese, grated
15ml/1 tbsp fresh chopped chervil
5ml/1 tsp fresh chopped marjoram
salt and freshly ground black pepper
5 large or 10 small sheets filo pastry
40–50g/1½–2oz butter, melted

1 Preheat the oven to 190°C/375°F/
Gas 5. Cook the spinach in a large
saucepan over a moderate heat for
3–4 minutes until the leaves have wilted,
shaking the saucepan occasionally.
Strain and press out the excess liquid.

2 Heat the oil and butter in a saucepan
and fry the onion for 3–4 minutes until
softened. Remove from the heat and add
half of the spinach. Combine, using a
metal spoon to break up the spinach.

3 Add the ricotta cheese and stir until
evenly combined. Stir in the remaining
spinach, again chopping it into the
mixture with a metal spoon. Fold in the
feta and Gruyère or Emmenthal cheese,
chervil, marjoram and seasoning.

4 Lay a sheet of filo pastry measuring
about 30cm/12 in square on a work surface. (If you have small filo sheets, lay
them side by side, overlapping by about
2.5cm/1in in the middle.) Brush with
melted butter and cover with a second
sheet; brush this with butter and build
up five layers of pastry in this way.

5 Spread the filling over the pastry,
leaving a 2.5cm/1in border. Fold the
sides inwards and then roll up.

6 Place the roll, seam side down, on a
greased baking sheet and brush with the
remaining butter. Bake in the oven for
about 30 minutes until golden brown.

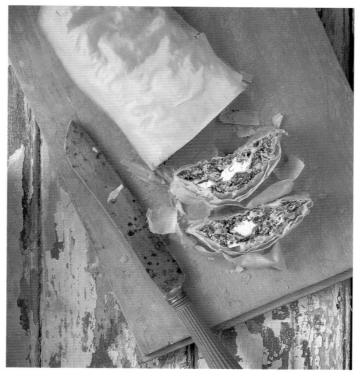

SPINACH RAVIOLI

HOME-MADE RAVIOLI IS TIME-CONSUMING, YET IT IS WORTH THE EFFORT AS EVEN THE BEST SHOP-BOUGHT PASTA NEVER TASTES QUITE AS FRESH. TO COMPLEMENT THIS EFFORT, MAKE THE FILLING EXACTLY TO YOUR LIKING, TASTING IT FOR THE RIGHT BALANCE OF SPINACH AND CHEESE.

SERVES FOUR

INGREDIENTS
225g/8oz fresh spinach
40g/1½oz butter
1 small onion, finely chopped
25g/1oz Parmesan cheese, grated
40g/1½oz dolcellate cheese, crumbled
15ml/1 tbsp chopped fresh parsley
salt and freshly ground black pepper
shavings of Parmesan cheese, to serve
For the pasta dough
350g/12oz strong white flour
4ml/¾ tsp salt
2 eggs
15ml/1 tbsp olive oil

1 To make the pasta dough, mix together the flour and salt in a large bowl or food processor. Add the eggs, olive oil and about 45ml/3 tbsp of cold water or enough to make a pliable dough. If working by hand, mix the ingredients together and then knead the dough for about 15 minutes until very smooth. Or, process for about 1½ minutes in a food processor. Place the dough in a plastic bag and chill for at least 1 hour (or overnight if more convenient).

2 Cook the spinach in a large, covered saucepan for 3–4 minutes, until the leaves have wilted. Strain and press out the excess liquid. Set aside to cool a little and then chop finely.

3 Melt half the butter in a small saucepan and fry the onion over a gentle heat for about 5–6 minutes until soft. Place in a bowl with the chopped spinach, the Parmesan and dolcellate cheeses, and seasoning. Mix well.

4 Grease a ravioli tin. Roll out half or a quarter of the pasta dough to a thickness of about 3mm/⅛in. Lay the dough over the ravioli tin, pressing it well into each of the squares.

5 Spoon a little spinach mixture into each cavity, then roll out a second piece of dough and lay it on top. Press a rolling pin evenly over the top of the tin to seal the edges and then cut the ravioli into squares using a pastry cutter.

6 Place the ravioli in a large saucepan of boiling water and simmer for about 4–5 minutes until cooked through but *al dente*. Drain well and then toss with the remaining butter and the parsley.

7 Divide between four serving plates and serve scattered with shavings of Parmesan cheese.

COOK'S TIP
For a small ravioli tin of 32 holes, divide the dough into quarters. Roll the dough out until it covers the tin comfortably – it takes some time but the pasta needs to be thin otherwise the ravioli will be too stodgy. For a large ravioli tin of 64 holes, divide the dough in half.

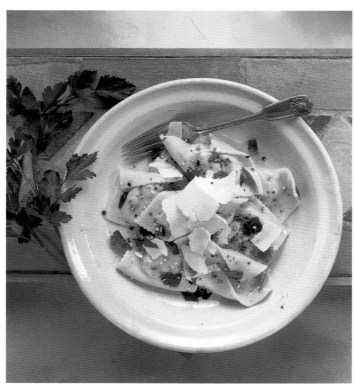

CAULIFLOWER, PRAWN AND BROCCOLI TEMPURA

ALL SORTS OF VEGETABLES ARE DELICIOUS DEEP FRIED JAPANESE-STYLE (TEMPURA). FIRM VEGETABLES, SUCH AS CAULIFLOWER AND BROCCOLI, ARE BEST BLANCHED BEFORE FRYING BUT MANGE-TOUT, RED AND GREEN PEPPER SLICES, AND MUSHROOMS CAN SIMPLY BE DIPPED IN THE BATTER AND FRIED.

SERVES FOUR

INGREDIENTS
½ cauliflower
275g/10oz broccoli
8 raw prawns
8 button mushrooms (optional)
sunflower or vegetable oil, for
  deep frying
lemon wedges and sprigs of coriander,
  to garnish (optional)
soy sauce, to serve
For the batter
  115g/4oz plain flour
  pinch of salt
  2 eggs, separated
  175ml/6fl oz/¾ cup iced water
  30ml/2 tbsp sunflower or vegetable oil

1 Cut the cauliflower and broccoli into medium-size florets. Blanch all the florets for 1–2 minutes. Drain. Refresh under cold running water. Put to one side. Peel the prawns but leave their tails intact. Put to one side.

2 To make the batter, place the flour and salt in a bowl, blend together the egg yolks and water and stir into the flour, beating well to make a smooth batter.

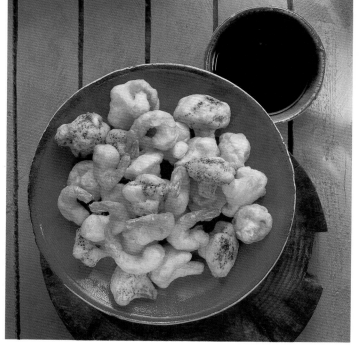

3 Beat in the oil and then whisk the egg whites until stiff and fold into the batter. Heat the oil for deep frying to 190°C/375°F. Coat a few of the vegetables and prawns in the batter.

4 Fry for 2–3 minutes until lightly golden and puffy. Transfer to a plate lined with kitchen paper and keep warm while frying the remaining tempura.

5 Arrange on individual plates, garnish with lemon and coriander, if liked, and serve with little bowls of soy sauce.

COOK'S TIP
Try cooking other vegetables in this way, such as aubergines and courgettes, or even the delicate young leaves of cauliflower, or celery leaves.

CAULIFLOWER AND MUSHROOM GOUGÈRE

THIS IS AN ALL-ROUND FAVOURITE VEGETARIAN DISH. WHEN COOKING THIS DISH FOR MEAT LOVERS, CHOPPED ROAST HAM OR FRIED BACON CAN BE ADDED.

SERVES FOUR TO SIX

INGREDIENTS
300ml/½ pint/1¼ cups water
115g/4oz butter or margarine
150g/5oz plain flour
4 eggs
115g/4oz Gruyère or Cheddar cheese,
   finely diced
5ml/1 tsp Dijon mustard
salt and freshly ground black pepper
For the filling
½ x 400g/14oz can tomatoes
15ml/1 tbsp sunflower oil
15g/½oz butter or margarine
1 onion, chopped
115g/4oz button mushrooms, halved
   if large
1 small cauliflower, broken into
   small florets
sprig of thyme
salt and freshly ground black pepper

1 Preheat the oven to 200°C/400°F/
Gas 6 and butter a large ovenproof dish.
Place the water and butter together in a
large saucepan and heat until the butter
has melted. Remove from the heat and
add all the flour at once. Beat well with a
wooden spoon for about 30 seconds until
smooth. Allow to cool slightly.

2 Beat in the eggs, one at a time, and
continue beating until the mixture is
thick and glossy. Stir in the cheese and
mustard and season with salt and
pepper. Spread the mixture around the
sides of the ovenproof dish, leaving a
hollow in the centre for the filling.

3 To make the filling, purée the
tomatoes in a blender or food processor
and then pour into a measuring jug. Add
enough water to make up to 300ml/
½ pint/1¼ cups of liquid.

4 Heat the oil and butter in a flameproof
casserole and fry the onion for about
3–4 minutes until softened but not
browned. Add the mushrooms and cook
for 2–3 minutes until they begin to be
flecked with brown. Add the cauliflower
florets and stir-fry for 1 minute.

5 Add the tomato liquid, thyme and
seasoning. Cook, uncovered, over a
gentle heat for about 5 minutes until the
cauliflower is only just tender.

6 Spoon the mixture into the hollow in
the ovenproof dish, adding all the liquid.
Bake in the oven for about 35–40
minutes, until the outer pastry is well
risen and golden brown.

COOK'S TIP
For a variation, ham or bacon can be
added. Use about 115–150g/4–5oz
thickly sliced roast ham and add to the
sauce at the end of step 5.

BALTI-STYLE CAULIFLOWER WITH TOMATOES

BALTI IS A TYPE OF MEAT AND VEGETABLE COOKING FROM PAKISTAN AND NORTHERN INDIA. IT CAN REFER BOTH TO THE PAN USED FOR COOKING, WHICH IS LIKE A LITTLE WOK, AND THE SPICES USED. IN THE ABSENCE OF A GENUINE BALTI PAN, USE EITHER A WOK OR A HEAVY FRYING PAN.

SERVES FOUR

INGREDIENTS
  30ml/2 tbsp vegetable oil
  1 onion, chopped
  2 garlic cloves, crushed
  1 cauliflower, broken into florets
  5ml/1 tsp ground coriander
  5ml/1 tsp ground cumin
  5ml/1 tsp ground fennel seeds
  2.5ml/½ tsp garam masala
  pinch of ground ginger
  2.5ml/½ tsp chilli powder
  4 plum tomatoes, peeled, seeded
    and quartered
  175ml/6fl oz/¾ cup water
  175g/6oz fresh spinach, roughly
    chopped
  15–30ml/1–2 tbsp lemon juice
  salt and freshly ground black
    pepper

1 Heat the oil in a balti pan, wok, or large frying pan. Add the onion and garlic and stir-fry for 2–3 minutes over a high heat until the onion begins to brown. Add the cauliflower florets and stir-fry for a further 2–3 minutes until the cauliflower is flecked with brown.

2 Add the coriander, cumin, fennel seeds, garam masala, ginger and chilli powder and cook over a high heat for 1 minute, stirring all the time; then add the tomatoes, water and salt and pepper. Bring to the boil and then reduce the heat, cover and simmer for 5–6 minutes until the cauliflower is just tender.

3 Stir in the chopped spinach, cover and cook for 1 minute until the spinach is tender. Add enough lemon juice to sharpen the flavour and adjust the seasoning to taste.

4 Serve straight from the pan, with an Indian meal or with chicken or meat.

HOT BROCCOLI TARTLETS

IN FRANCE, HOME OF THE CLASSIC QUICHE LORRAINE, YOU CAN ALSO FIND A WHOLE VARIETY OF SAVOURY TARTLETS, FILLED WITH ONIONS, LEEKS, MUSHROOMS AND BROCCOLI. THIS VERSION IS SIMPLE TO PREPARE AND WOULD MAKE AN ELEGANT START TO A MEAL.

MAKES EIGHT TO TEN

INGREDIENTS
    15ml/1 tbsp oil
    1 leek, finely sliced
    175g/6oz broccoli, broken into florets
    15g/½oz butter
    15g/½oz plain flour
    150ml/¼ pint/⅔ cup milk
    50g/2oz goat's Cheddar or farmhouse
      Cheddar, grated
    fresh chervil, to garnish
For the pastry
    175g/6oz plain flour
    75g/3oz butter
    1 egg
    pinch of salt

1 To make the pastry, place the flour and salt in a large bowl and rub in the butter and egg to make a dough. Add a little cold water if necessary, knead lightly, then wrap in clear film and leave to rest in the fridge for 1 hour.

2 Preheat the oven to 190°C/375°F/ Gas 5. Let the dough return to room temperature for 10 minutes and then roll out on a lightly floured surface and line 8–10 deep patty tins. Prick the bases with a fork and bake in the oven for about 10–15 minutes until the pastry is firm and lightly golden. Increase the oven temperature to 200°C/400°F/Gas 6.

3 Heat the oil in a small saucepan and sauté the leek for 4–5 minutes until soft. Add the broccoli, stir-fry for about 1 minute and then add a little water. Cover and steam for 3–4 minutes until the broccoli is just tender.

4 Melt the butter in a separate saucepan, stir in the flour and cook for a minute, stirring all the time. Slowly add the milk and stir to make a smooth sauce. Add half of the cheese and season with salt and pepper.

5 Spoon a little broccoli and leek into each tartlet case and then spoon over the sauce. Sprinkle each tartlet with the remaining cheese and then bake in the oven for about 10 minutes until golden.

6 Serve the tartlets as part of a buffet or as a starter, garnished with chervil.

CHARD PASTIES

CHARD, LIKE SPINACH, GOES PARTICULARLY WELL IN PASTIES. UNLIKE SOME GREEN VEGETABLES, IT CAN SURVIVE A LITTLE EXTRA COOKING AND IS SUBSTANTIAL ENOUGH TO BE THE PRINCIPAL INGREDIENT. FOR A MORE SAVOURY PASTRY, REPLACE A LITTLE OF THE BUTTER WITH GRATED CHEESE.

SERVES FOUR

INGREDIENTS
     675g/1½lb Swiss chard
     25g/1oz butter or margarine
     1 onion, finely chopped
     75g/3oz streaky bacon, chopped
     50g/2oz Gruyère cheese, grated
     25g/1oz fresh brown or white
        breadcrumbs
     90ml/6 tbsp single cream
     salt and freshly ground black pepper
For the pastry
     275g/10oz plain flour
     150g/5oz butter or margarine
     pinch of salt
     beaten egg for glazing

1 To make the pastry, place the flour and salt in a mixing bowl and rub in the butter or margarine. Add a little cold water and mix to a soft dough. Knead lightly on a floured surface. Wrap in clear film and chill for 30 minutes.

2 Trim the stalks of the chard and then chop both the leaves and stalk. Place in a heavy-based pan, cover and cook over a low heat for 6–8 minutes until the stalks are tender and the leaves wilted. Shake the pan occasionally. Strain and press out the excess liquid, then place in a mixing bowl and leave to cool.

3 Melt the butter in a small frying pan and fry the onion and bacon for about 4–5 minutes until the onion is lightly golden and the bacon browned.

4 Add the onion and bacon to the chard and stir in the cheese, breadcrumbs, cream and seasoning to taste. Preheat the oven to 200°C/400°F/Gas 6.

5 Divide the pastry into four and roll out into rounds. Spoon the filling on to the centre of each and dampen the edges with water. Bring the sides together over the filling and press together to seal. Brush with beaten egg and then put on an oiled baking sheet. Bake for about 15–20 minutes until the pastry is golden.

CRUNCHY CABBAGE SALAD WITH PESTO MAYONNAISE

Both the pesto and the mayonnaise can be made for this dish. However, if time is short, you can buy them both ready-prepared and it will taste just as good. Add the dressing just before serving to prevent the cabbage going soggy.

SERVES FOUR TO SIX

INGREDIENTS
    1 small or ½ medium white cabbage
    3–4 carrots, grated
    4 spring onions, finely sliced
    25–40g/1–1½oz pine nuts
    15ml/1 tbsp chopped fresh mixed
      herbs; parsley, basil and chervil
For the pesto mayonnaise
    1 egg yolk
    about 10ml/2 tsp lemon juice
    200ml/7fl oz/⅞ cup sunflower oil
    10ml/2 tsp pesto
    60ml/4 tbsp natural yogurt
    salt and freshly ground black pepper

1 To make the mayonnaise, place the egg yolk in a blender or food processor and process with the lemon juice. With the machine running, very slowly add the oil, pouring it more quickly as the mayonnaise emulsifies. Season to taste with salt and pepper and a little more lemon juice if necessary. Alternatively, make by hand using a balloon whisk.

2 Spoon 75ml/5 tbsp of mayonnaise into a bowl and stir in the pesto and yogurt, beating well to make a fairly thin dressing. (The remaining mayonnaise will keep for about 3–4 weeks in a screw-top jar in the fridge.)

3 Using a food processor or a sharp knife, thinly slice the cabbage and place in a large salad bowl.

4 Add the carrots and spring onions, together with the pine nuts and herbs, mixing thoroughly with your hands. Stir the pesto dressing into the salad or serve separately in a small dish if preferred.

PASTA WITH SAVOY CABBAGE AND GRUYÈRE

THIS IS AN INEXPENSIVE AND SIMPLE DISH WITH A SURPRISING TEXTURE AND FLAVOUR. THE CABBAGE IS COOKED SO THAT IT HAS PLENTY OF "BITE" TO IT, CONTRASTING WITH THE SOFTNESS OF THE PASTA.

SERVES FOUR

INGREDIENTS

1 small Savoy or green cabbage, thinly sliced
25g/1oz butter
1 small onion, chopped
350g/12oz pasta, e.g. tagliatelle, fettucine or penne
15ml/1 tbsp chopped fresh parsley
150ml/¼ pint/⅔ cup single cream
50g/2oz Gruyère or Cheddar cheese, grated
about 300ml/½ pint/1¼ cups hot vegetable or chicken stock
salt and freshly ground black pepper

1 Preheat the oven to 180°C/350°F/ Gas 4 and butter a large casserole. Place the cabbage in a mixing bowl.

2 Melt the butter in a small frying pan and fry the onion until softened. Stir into the cabbage in the bowl.

3 Cook the pasta according to the instructions, until *al dente*.

4 Drain well and stir into the bowl with the cabbage and onion. Add the parsley and mix well and then pour into the prepared casserole.

5 Beat together the cream and Gruyère or Cheddar cheese and then stir in the hot stock. Season well and pour over the cabbage and pasta, so that it comes about halfway up the casserole. If necessary, add a little more stock.

6 Cover tightly with foil or a lid and cook in the oven for 30–35 minutes, until the cabbage is tender and the stock is bubbling. Remove the lid for the last 5 minutes of the cooking time to brown the top.

TURNIP TOPS WITH PARMESAN AND GARLIC

TURNIP TOPS HAVE A PRONOUNCED FLAVOUR AND ARE GOOD WHEN COOKED WITH OTHER STRONG-FLAVOURED INGREDIENTS SUCH AS ONIONS, GARLIC AND PARMESAN CHEESE. THEY DO NOT NEED LONG COOKING AS THE LEAVES ARE QUITE TENDER.

SERVES FOUR

INGREDIENTS
45ml/3 tbsp olive oil
2 garlic cloves, crushed
4 spring onions, sliced
350g/12oz turnip tops, thinly sliced,
   tough stalk removed
50g/2oz Parmesan cheese, grated
salt and freshly ground black pepper
shavings of Parmesan cheese,
   to garnish

1 Heat the olive oil in a large saucepan and fry the garlic for a few seconds. Add the spring onions, stir-fry for 2 minutes and then add the turnip tops.

2 Stir-fry for a few minutes so that the greens are coated in oil, then add about 50ml/2fl oz/¼ cup water. Bring to the boil, cover and simmer until the greens are tender. Stir occasionally and do not allow the pan to boil dry.

3 Bring the liquid to the boil and allow the excess to evaporate and then stir in the Parmesan cheese. Serve at once with extra shavings of cheese, if liked.

KOHLRABI STUFFED WITH PEPPERS

IF YOU HAVEN'T SAMPLED KOHLRABI, OR HAVE ONLY EATEN IT IN STEWS WHERE ITS FLAVOUR IS LOST, THIS DISH IS RECOMMENDED. THE SLIGHTLY SHARP FLAVOUR OF THE PEPPERS IS AN EXCELLENT FOIL TO THE MORE EARTHY FLAVOUR OF THE KOHLRABI.

SERVES FOUR

INGREDIENTS

4 small kohlrabi, about 175–225g/
  6–8oz each
about 400ml/14fl oz/1⅔ cups hot
  vegetable stock
15ml/1 tbsp olive or sunflower oil
1 onion, chopped
1 small red pepper, seeded and sliced
1 small green pepper, seeded
  and sliced
salt and freshly ground black pepper
flat leaf parsley, to garnish (optional)

1 Preheat the oven to 180°C/350°F/
Gas 4. Trim and top and tail the kohlrabi
and arrange in the base of a medium-
size ovenproof dish.

2 Pour over the stock to come about
halfway up the vegetables. Cover and
braise in the oven for about 30 minutes
until tender. Transfer to a plate and allow
to cool, reserving the stock.

3 Heat the oil in a frying pan and fry the
onion for 3–4 minutes over a gentle heat,
stirring occasionally. Add the peppers
and cook for a further 2–3 minutes, until
the onion is lightly browned.

4 Add the reserved vegetable stock
and a little seasoning, then simmer,
uncovered, over a moderate heat until
the stock has almost evaporated.

5 Scoop out the flesh from the kohlrabi
and roughly chop. Stir the flesh into the
onion and pepper mixture, taste and
adjust the seasoning. Arrange the shells
in a shallow ovenproof dish.

6 Spoon the filling into the kohlrabi
shells. Place in the oven for 5–10 minutes to heat through and then serve,
garnished with flat leaf parsley, if liked.

STIR-FRIED BRUSSELS SPROUTS

SERVES FOUR

INGREDIENTS

450g/1lb Brussels sprouts
15ml/1 tbsp sunflower oil
6–8 spring onions, cut into 2.5cm/
  1 in lengths
2 slices fresh root ginger
40g/1½oz slivered almonds
150–175ml/5–6fl oz/⅔–¾ cup
  vegetable or chicken stock
salt

1 Remove any large outer leaves and trim the bases of the Brussels sprouts. Cut into slices about 7mm/⅓in thick.

2 Heat the oil in a wok or heavy frying pan and fry the spring onions and the ginger for 2–3 minutes, stirring frequently. Add the almonds and stir-fry over a moderate heat until both the onions and almonds begin to brown.

3 Remove and discard the ginger, reduce the heat and stir in the Brussels sprouts. Stir-fry for a few minutes and then pour in the stock and cook over a gentle heat for 5–6 minutes or until the sprouts are nearly tender.

4 Add a little salt, if necessary, and then increase the heat to boil off the excess liquid. Spoon into a warmed serving dish and serve immediately.

BRUSSELS SPROUTS GRATIN

SERVES FOUR

INGREDIENTS

15g/½oz butter
150ml/¼ pint/⅔ cup whipping cream
150ml/¼ pint/⅔ cup milk
25g/1oz Parmesan cheese, grated
675g/1½lb Brussels sprouts, thinly
  sliced
1 garlic clove, finely chopped
salt and freshly ground black pepper

1 Preheat the oven to 150°C/300°F/ Gas 2 and butter a shallow ovenproof dish. Blend together the cream, milk, Parmesan cheese and seasoning.

2 Place a layer of Brussels sprouts in the base of the prepared dish, sprinkle with a little garlic and pour over about a quarter of the cream mixture. Add another layer of sprouts and continue building layers in this way, ending with the remaining cream and milk.

3 Cover loosely with greaseproof paper and bake for 1–1¼hours. Halfway through cooking, remove the paper and press the sprouts under the liquid in the dish. Return to the oven to brown.

PAK-CHOI <u>WITH</u> LIME DRESSING

FOR THIS THAI RECIPE, THE COCONUT DRESSING IS TRADITIONALLY MADE USING FISH SAUCE, BUT VEGETARIANS COULD USE MUSHROOM SAUCE INSTEAD. BEWARE, THIS IS A FIERY DISH!

SERVES FOUR

INGREDIENTS
  6 spring onions
  2 pak-choi
  30ml/2 tbsp oil
  3 fresh red chillies, cut into thin
    strips
  4 garlic cloves, thinly sliced
  15ml/1 tbsp crushed peanuts
For the dressing
  15–30ml/1–2 tbsp fish sauce
  30ml/2 tbsp lime juice
  250ml/8fl oz/1 cup coconut milk

1 To make the dressing, blend together the fish sauce and lime juice, and then stir in the coconut milk.

2 Cut the spring onions diagonally into slices, including all but the very tips of the green parts.

3 Using a large sharp knife, cut the pak-choi into very fine shreds.

4 Heat the oil in a wok and stir-fry the chillies for 2–3 minutes until crisp. Transfer to a plate using a slotted spoon.

5 Stir-fry the garlic for 30–60 seconds until golden brown and transfer to the plate with the chillies.

6 Stir-fry the white parts of the spring onions for about 2–3 minutes and then add the green parts and stir-fry for a further 1 minute. Add to the plate with the chillies and garlic.

7 Bring a large pan of salted water to the boil and add the pak-choi; stir twice and then drain immediately.

8 Place the warmed pak-choi in a large bowl, add the coconut dressing and stir well. Spoon into a large serving bowl and sprinkle with the crushed peanuts and the stir-fried chilli mixture. Serve either warm or cold.

COOK'S TIP
Coconut milk is available in cans from large supermarkets and Chinese stores. Alternatively, creamed coconut is available in packets. To use creamed coconut, place about 115g/4oz in a jug and pour over 250ml/8fl oz/1 cup boiling water. Stir well until dissolved.

DOLMADES

*DOLMADES ARE STUFFED VINE LEAVES, A TRADITIONAL GREEK DISH. IF YOU CAN'T OBTAIN FRESH VINE
LEAVES, USE A PACKET OF BRINED VINE LEAVES. SOAK THE LEAVES IN HOT WATER FOR 20 MINUTES THEN
RINSE AND DRY WELL ON KITCHEN PAPER BEFORE USE.*

MAKES 20–24

INGREDIENTS

20–30 fresh young vine leaves
30ml/2 tbsp olive oil
1 large onion, finely chopped
1 garlic clove, crushed
225g/8oz cooked long grain rice,
   or mixed white and wild rice
about 45ml/3 tbsp pine nuts
15ml/1 tbsp flaked almonds
40g/1½oz sultanas
15ml/ 1 tbsp snipped chives
15ml/ 1 tbsp finely chopped
   fresh mint
juice of ½ lemon
150ml/¼ pint/⅔ cup white wine
hot vegetable stock
salt and freshly ground black pepper
sprig of mint, to garnish
Greek yogurt, to serve

1 Bring a large pan of water to the boil
and cook the vine leaves for about
2–3 minutes. They will darken and go
limp after about 1 minute and simmering
for a further minute or so ensures they
are pliable. If using leaves from a packet,
place them in a large bowl, cover with
boiling water and leave for a few minutes
until the leaves can be easily separated.
Rinse them under cold water and drain
on kitchen paper.

2 Heat the oil in a small frying pan and
fry the onion and garlic for 3–4 minutes
over a gentle heat until soft.

3 Spoon the onion and garlic mixture
into a bowl and add the cooked rice.

4 Stir in 30ml/2 tbsp of the pine nuts,
the almonds, sultanas, chives, mint,
lemon juice and seasoning and mix well.

5 Lay a vine leaf on a clean work surface, veined side uppermost. Place a
spoonful of filling near the stem, fold the
lower part of the leaf over it and roll up,
folding in the sides as you go. Continue
stuffing the vine leaves in the same way.

6 Line the base of a deep frying pan
with four large vine leaves. Place the
stuffed vine leaves close together in the
pan, seam side down, in a single layer.

7 Add the wine and enough stock to just
cover the vine leaves. Place a plate
directly over the leaves, then cover and
simmer gently for 30 minutes, checking
to make sure the pan does not boil dry.

8 Chill the vine leaves, then serve
garnished with the remaining pine nuts,
a sprig of mint and a little yogurt.

PEAS WITH BABY ONIONS AND CREAM

IDEALLY, USE FRESH PEAS AND FRESH BABY ONIONS. FROZEN PEAS ARE AN ACCEPTABLE SUBSTITUTE IF FRESH ONES AREN'T AVAILABLE, BUT FROZEN ONIONS TEND TO BE INSIPID AND ARE NOT WORTH USING. ALTERNATIVELY, USE THE WHITE PARTS OF SPRING ONIONS.

SERVES FOUR

INGREDIENTS
175g/6oz baby onions
15g/½ oz butter
900g/2lb fresh peas (about
    350g/12oz shelled or frozen)
150ml/¼ pint/⅔ cup double cream
15g/½oz plain flour
10ml/2 tsp chopped fresh parsley
15–30ml/1–2 tbsp lemon juice
    (optional)
salt and freshly ground black pepper

1 Peel the onions and halve them if necessary. Melt the butter in a flame-proof casserole and fry the onions for 5–6 minutes over a moderate heat, until they begin to be flecked with brown.

3 Using a small whisk, blend the cream with the flour. Remove the pan from the heat and stir in the combined cream and flour, parsley and seasoning to taste.

4 Cook over a gentle heat for about 3–4 minutes, until the sauce is thick. Taste and adjust the seasoning; add a little lemon juice to sharpen, if liked.

2 Add the peas and stir-fry for a few minutes. Add 120ml/4fl oz/¼ cup water and bring to the boil. Partially cover and simmer for about 10 minutes until both the peas and onions are tender. There should be a thin layer of water on the base of the pan – add a little more water if necessary or, if there is too much liquid, remove the lid and increase the heat until the liquid is reduced.

MANGE-TOUT WITH CHICKEN AND CORIANDER

MANGE-TOUT ARE SO DELICATE AND FRESH-TASTING THAT IT SEEMS A CRIME TO DO ANYTHING AT ALL WITH THEM, BARRING FLASH COOKING AND SERVING THEM HOT OR COLD WITH A LITTLE BUTTER OR A VINAIGRETTE DRESSING. THEY ARE EXCELLENT IN STIR-FRIES, ADDING COLOUR AND TEXTURE.

SERVES FOUR

INGREDIENTS
4 boned and skinned chicken breasts
225g/8oz mange-tout
45ml/3 tbsp vegetable oil, plus
 oil for deep frying
3 garlic cloves, finely chopped
2.5cm/1in piece fresh root ginger,
 freshly grated
5–6 spring onions, cut into 4cm/
 1½in lengths
10ml/2 tsp sesame oil
For the marinade
5ml/1 tsp cornflour
15ml/1 tbsp light soy sauce
15ml/1 tbsp medium dry sherry
15ml/1 tbsp vegetable oil
For the sauce
5ml/1 tsp cornflour
10–15ml/2–3 tsp dark soy sauce
120ml/4fl oz/½ cup chicken stock
30ml/2 tbsp oyster sauce
boiled rice, to serve

1 Cut the chicken into strips about 1 x 4cm/½ x 1½in. To make the marinade, blend together the cornflour and soy sauce. Stir in the sherry and oil. Pour over the chicken, turning the pieces over to coat evenly, and leave for 30 minutes.

2 Trim the mange-tout and plunge into a pan of boiling salted water. Bring back to the boil and then drain and refresh them under cold running water.

3 To make the sauce, mix together the cornflour, soy sauce, stock and oyster sauce and set aside.

4 Heat the oil in a deep fryer. Drain the chicken strips and fry, in batches if necessary, for about 30 seconds to brown. Drain and transfer to a plate using a slotted spoon.

5 Heat 15ml/1 tbsp of the vegetable oil in a wok and add the garlic and ginger. Stir-fry for 30 seconds. Add the mange-tout and stir-fry for 1–2 minutes. Transfer to a plate and keep warm.

6 Heat the remaining vegetable oil in the wok, add the spring onions and stir-fry for 1–2 minutes. Add the chicken and stir-fry for 2 minutes. Pour in the sauce, reduce the heat and cook until it thickens and the chicken is cooked through.

7 Stir in the sesame oil, and pour over the mange-tout. Serve with boiled rice.

FRENCH BEAN SALAD

ALTHOUGH BEAN SALADS ARE DELICIOUS SERVED WITH A SIMPLE VINAIGRETTE DRESSING, THIS DISH IS A LITTLE MORE ELABORATE. IT DOES, HOWEVER, ENHANCE THE FRESH FLAVOUR OF THE BEANS.

SERVES FOUR

INGREDIENTS
    450g/1lb French beans
    15ml/1 tbsp olive oil
    25g/1oz butter
    ½ garlic clove, crushed
    50g/2oz fresh white breadcrumbs
    15ml/1 tbsp chopped fresh
      parsley
    1 egg, hard-boiled and finely chopped
For the dressing
    30ml/2 tbsp olive oil
    30ml/2 tbsp sunflower oil
    10ml/2 tsp white wine vinegar
    ½ garlic clove, crushed
    1.5ml/¼ tsp French mustard
    pinch of sugar
    pinch of salt

1 Trim the French beans and cook in boiling salted water for 5–6 minutes until tender. Drain the beans and refresh them under cold running water and place in a serving bowl.

2 Make the salad dressing by blending the oils, vinegar, garlic, mustard, sugar and salt thoroughly together. Pour over the beans and toss to mix.

COOK'S TIP
For a more substantial salad, boil about 450g/1lb scrubbed new potatoes until tender, cool and then cut them into bite-size chunks. Stir into the French beans and then add the dressing.

3 Heat the oil and butter in a frying pan and fry the garlic for 1 minute. Stir in the breadcrumbs and fry over a moderate heat for about 3–4 minutes until golden brown, stirring frequently.

4 Remove the pan from the heat and stir in the parsley and then the egg. Sprinkle the breadcrumb mixture over the French beans. Serve warm or at room temperature.

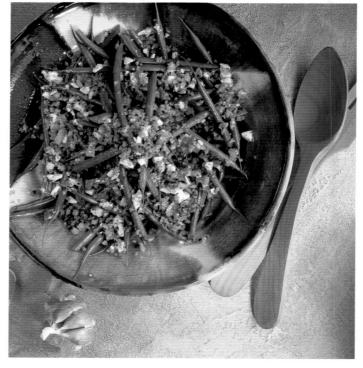

FRENCH BEANS WITH BACON AND CREAM

SERVES FOUR

INGREDIENTS
   350g/12oz French beans
   50–75g/2–3oz bacon, chopped
   25g/1oz butter or margarine
   15ml/1 tbsp plain flour
   350ml/12fl oz/1½ cups milk
     and single cream, mixed
   salt and freshly ground black pepper

2 Dry-fry the bacon until crisp, crumble into very small pieces and stir into the beans.

3 Melt the butter or margarine in a saucepan, stir in the flour and then add the milk and cream to make a smooth sauce. Season well with salt and pepper.

4 Pour the sauce over the beans and carefully mix it in. Cover lightly with a piece of foil and bake in the oven for 15–20 minutes until hot.

1 Preheat the oven to 190°C/375°F/Gas 5. Trim the beans and cook in lightly salted boiling water for about 5 minutes until just tender. Drain and place them in an ovenproof dish.

RUNNER BEANS WITH GARLIC

DELICATE AND FRESH-TASTING FLAGEOLET BEANS AND GARLIC ADD A DISTINCT FRENCH FLAVOUR TO THIS SIMPLE SIDE DISH. SERVE TO ACCOMPANY ROAST LAMB OR VEAL.

SERVES FOUR

INGREDIENTS
225g/8oz flageolet beans
15ml/1 tbsp olive oil
25g/1oz butter
1 onion, finely chopped
1–2 garlic cloves, crushed
3–4 tomatoes, peeled and chopped
350g/12oz runner beans, prepared
   and sliced
150ml/¼ pint/⅔ cup white wine
150ml/¼ pint/⅔ cup vegetable stock
30ml/2 tbsp chopped fresh parsley
salt and freshly ground black pepper

1 Place the flageolet beans in a large saucepan of water, bring to the boil and simmer for ¾–1 hour until tender. Drain.

2 Heat the oil and butter in a large frying pan and sauté the onion and garlic for 3–4 minutes until soft. Add the chopped tomatoes and continue cooking over a gentle heat until they are soft.

3 Stir the flageolet beans into the onion and tomato mixture, then add the runner beans, wine, stock, and a little salt. Stir well. Cover and simmer for 5–10 minutes until the runner beans are tender.

4 Increase the heat to reduce the liquid, then stir in the parsley and season with a little more salt, if necessary, and pepper.

INDIAN–STYLE OKRA

WHEN OKRA (BHINDI) IS SERVED IN INDIAN RESTAURANTS IT IS OFTEN FLAT AND SOGGY BECAUSE IT HAS BEEN OVERCOOKED OR LEFT STANDING. HOWEVER, WHEN YOU MAKE THIS DISH YOURSELF, YOU WILL REALIZE HOW DELICIOUS OKRA CAN BE.

SERVES FOUR

INGREDIENTS

   350g/12oz okra
   2 small onions
   2 garlic cloves, crushed
   1cm/½in piece fresh root ginger
   1 green chilli, seeded
   10ml/2 tsp ground cumin
   10ml/2 tsp ground coriander
   30ml/2 tbsp vegetable oil
   juice of 1 lemon

3 Reduce the heat and add the garlic and ginger mixture. Cook for about 2–3 minutes, stirring frequently, and then add the okra, lemon juice and 105ml/7 tbsp water. Stir well, cover tightly and simmer over a low heat for about 10 minutes until tender. Transfer to a serving dish, sprinkle with the fried onion rings and serve at once.

1 Trim the okra and cut into 1cm/½in lengths. Roughly chop one of the onions and place in a food processor or blender with the garlic, ginger, chilli and 90ml/6 tbsp water. Process to a paste. Add the cumin and coriander and blend again.

2 Thinly slice the remaining onion into half rings and fry in the oil for 6–8 minutes until golden brown. Transfer to a plate using a slotted spoon.

SWEETCORN AND CHEESE PASTIES

THESE TASTY PASTIES ARE REALLY SIMPLE TO MAKE AND EXTREMELY MOREISH — WHY NOT MAKE DOUBLE THE AMOUNT — THEY'LL GO LIKE HOT CAKES.

MAKES EIGHTEEN TO TWENTY

INGREDIENTS
    250g/9oz sweetcorn
    115g/4oz feta cheese
    1 egg, beaten
    30ml/2 tbsp whipping cream
    15g/½oz Parmesan cheese, grated
    3 spring onions, chopped
    8–10 small sheets filo pastry
    115g/4oz butter, melted
    freshly ground black pepper

1 Preheat the oven to 190°C/375°F/ Gas 5 and butter two patty tins.

2 If using fresh sweetcorn, strip the kernels from the cob using a sharp knife and simmer in a little salted water for 3–5 minutes until tender. For canned sweetcorn, drain and rinse well under cold running water.

3 Crumble the feta cheese into a bowl and stir in the sweetcorn. Add the egg, cream, Parmesan cheese, spring onions and ground black pepper, and stir well.

4 Take one sheet of pastry and cut it in half to make a square. (Keep the remaining pastry covered with a damp cloth to prevent it drying out.) Brush with melted butter and then fold into four, to make a smaller square (about 7.5cm/3in).

5 Place a heaped teaspoon of mixture in the centre of each pastry square and then squeeze the pastry around the filling to make a "money bag" casing.

6 Continue making pasties until all the mixture is used up. Brush the outside of each "bag" with any remaining butter and then bake in the oven for about 15 minutes until golden. Serve hot.

SWEETCORN AND SCALLOP CHOWDER

FRESH HOME-GROWN SWEETCORN IS IDEAL FOR THIS CHOWDER, ALTHOUGH CANNED OR FROZEN SWEET-CORN ALSO WORKS WELL. THIS SOUP IS ALMOST A MEAL IN ITSELF AND MAKES A PERFECT LUNCH DISH.

SERVES FOUR TO SIX

INGREDIENTS

2 ears of corn or 200g/7oz frozen
   or canned sweetcorn
600ml/1 pint/2½ cups milk
15g/½oz butter or margarine
1 small leek or onion, chopped
40g/1½oz smoked streaky bacon,
   finely chopped
1 small garlic clove, crushed
1 small green pepper, seeded
   and diced
1 celery stalk, chopped
1 medium potato, diced
15ml/1 tbsp plain flour
300ml/½ pint/1¼ cups chicken
   or vegetable stock
4 scallops
115g/4oz cooked fresh mussels
pinch of paprika
150ml/¼ pint/⅔ cup single cream
   (optional)
salt and freshly ground black pepper

1 Using a sharp knife, slice down the ears of the corn to remove the kernels. Place half of the kernels in a food processor or blender and process with a little of the milk.

2 Melt the butter or margarine in a large saucepan and gently fry the leek or onion, bacon and garlic for 4–5 minutes until the leek is soft but not browned. Add the green pepper, celery and potato and sweat over a gentle heat for a further 3–4 minutes, stirring frequently.

3 Stir in the flour and cook for about 1–2 minutes until the mixture is golden and frothy. Gradually stir in the milk and corn mixture, stock, the remaining milk and corn kernels and seasoning.

4 Bring to the boil and then reduce the heat to a gentle simmer, and cook, partially covered, for 15–20 minutes until the vegetables are tender.

5 Pull the corals away from the scallops and slice the white flesh into 5mm/¼in slices. Stir the scallops into the soup, cook for 4 minutes and then stir in the corals, mussels and paprika. Allow to heat through for a few minutes and then stir in the cream, if using. Adjust the seasoning to taste and serve.

SQUASH RECIPES

ONION SQUASH RISOTTO

SERVES FOUR

INGREDIENTS

   1 onion squash or pumpkin, about
     900g–1kg/2–2¼lb
   30ml/2 tbsp olive oil
   1 onion, chopped
   1–2 garlic cloves, crushed
   115g/4oz streaky bacon, chopped
   115g/4oz arborio rice
   600–750ml/1–1¼ pints/2½–3 cups
     chicken stock
   40g/1½oz Parmesan cheese, grated
   15ml/1 tbsp chopped fresh parsley
   salt and freshly ground black pepper

1 Halve or quarter the onion squash or
pumpkin, remove the seeds and skin,
and then cut into chunks about 1–2cm/
½–¾in in size.

2 Heat the oil in a flameproof casserole
and fry the onion and garlic for about
3–4 minutes, stirring frequently. Add the
bacon and continue frying until both the
onion and bacon are lightly golden.

3 Add the squash or pumpkin, stir-fry
for a few minutes. Add the rice and cook
for about 2 minutes, stirring all the time.

4 Pour in about half of the stock and
season. Stir well and then half cover and
simmer gently for about 20 minutes,
stirring occasionally. As the liquid is
absorbed, add more stock and stir to
prevent the mixture sticking to the base.

5 When the squash and rice are nearly
tender, add a little more stock. Cook,
uncovered for 5–10 minutes. Stir in the
Parmesan cheese and parsley and serve.

PUMPKIN SOUP

*THE SWEET FLAVOUR OF PUMPKIN IS GOOD IN SOUPS, TEAMING WELL WITH OTHER MORE SAVOURY
INGREDIENTS SUCH AS ONIONS AND POTATOES TO MAKE A WARM AND COMFORTING DISH.*

SERVES FOUR TO SIX

INGREDIENTS

   15ml/1 tbsp sunflower oil
   25g/1oz butter
   1 large onion, sliced
   675g/1½lb pumpkin, cut into
     large chunks
   450g/1lb potatoes, sliced
   600ml/1 pint/2½ cups vegetable stock
   good pinch of nutmeg
   5ml/1 tsp chopped fresh tarragon
   600ml/1 pint/2½ cups milk
   about 5–10ml/1–2 tsp lemon juice
   salt and freshly ground black pepper

1 Heat the oil and butter in a heavy-
based saucepan and fry the onion for
4–5 minutes over a gentle heat until soft
but not browned, stirring frequently.

2 Add the pumpkin and potato, stir well
and then cover and sweat over a low heat
for about 10 minutes until the vegetables
are almost tender, stirring occasionally to
prevent them from sticking to the pan.

3 Stir in the stock, nutmeg, tarragon
and seasoning. Bring to the boil and then
simmer for about 10 minutes until the
vegetables are completely tender.

4 Allow to cool slightly, then pour into a
food processor or blender and process
until smooth. Pour back into a clean
saucepan and add the milk. Heat gently
and then taste, adding the lemon juice
and extra seasoning if necessary. Serve
piping hot with crusty brown bread.

BAKED COURGETTES

WHEN VERY SMALL AND VERY FRESH COURGETTES ARE USED FOR THIS RECIPE IT IS WONDERFUL, BOTH SIMPLE AND DELICIOUS. THE CREAMY YET TANGY GOAT'S CHEESE CONTRASTS WELL WITH THE VERY DELICATE FLAVOUR OF THE YOUNG COURGETTES.

SERVES FOUR

INGREDIENTS

    8 small courgettes, about 450g/1lb
      total weight
    15ml/1 tbsp olive oil, plus extra
      for greasing
    75–115g/3–4oz goat's cheese, cut
      into thin strips
    small bunch fresh mint, finely
      chopped   ·
    freshly ground black pepper

1 Preheat the oven to 180°C/350°F/ Gas 4. Cut out eight rectangles of foil large enough to encase each courgette and brush each with a little oil.

2 Trim the courgettes and cut a thin slit along the length of each.

3 Insert pieces of goat's cheese in the slits. Add a little mint and sprinkle with the olive oil and black pepper.

4 Wrap each courgette in the foil rectangles, place on a baking sheet and bake for about 25 minutes until tender.

COOK'S TIP
Almost any cheese could be used in this recipe. Mild cheeses, however, such as a mild cheddar or mozzarella, will best allow the flavour of the courgettes to be appreciated.

COURGETTES ITALIAN-STYLE

*USE A GOOD QUALITY OLIVE OIL AND SUNFLOWER OIL THE OLIVE OIL GIVES IT A DELICIOUS
FRAGRANCY BUT IS NOT ALLOWED TO OVERPOWER THE COURGETTES.*

SERVES FOUR

INGREDIENTS
15ml/1 tbsp olive oil
15ml/1 tbsp sunflower oil
1 large onion, chopped
1 garlic clove, crushed
4–5 medium courgettes, cut into
   1cm/½in slices
150ml/¼ pint/⅔ cup chicken
   or vegetable stock
2.5ml/½ tsp fresh chopped oregano
salt and freshly ground black pepper
chopped fresh parsley, to garnish

3 Stir in the stock, oregano and seasoning and simmer gently for 8–10 minutes,
until the liquid has almost evaporated.
Spoon the courgettes into a serving dish,
sprinkle with parsley and serve.

1 Heat the oils in a large frying pan and
fry the onion and garlic over a moderate
heat for 5–6 minutes until the onion has
softened and is beginning to brown.

2 Add the courgettes and fry for about
4 minutes until they just begin to be
flecked with brown. Stir frequently.

MARROWS WITH GNOCCHI

A SIMPLE WAY WITH MARROW, THIS DISH MAKES AN EXCELLENT ACCOMPANIMENT TO GRILLED MEAT BUT IT IS ALSO GOOD WITH A VEGETARIAN DISH, OR SIMPLY SERVED WITH GRILLED TOMATOES. GNOCCHI ARE AVAILABLE FROM MOST SUPERMARKETS; ITALIAN DELICATESSENS MAY ALSO SELL FRESH GNOCCHI.

SERVES FOUR

INGREDIENTS
  1 small marrow, cut into
    bite-size chunks
  50g/2oz butter
  400g/14oz packet gnocchi
  ½ garlic clove, crushed
  salt and freshly ground black pepper
  chopped fresh basil, to garnish

1 Preheat the oven to 180°C/350°F/ Gas 4 and butter a large ovenproof dish. Place the marrow, more or less in a single layer, in the dish. Dot all over with the remaining butter.

2 Place a double piece of buttered greaseproof paper over the top. Cover with an ovenproof plate or lid so that it presses the marrow down, and then place a heavy, ovenproof weight on top of that. (Use a couple of old-fashioned scale weights.)

3 Put in the oven to bake for about 15 minutes, by which time the marrow should just be tender.

4 Cook the gnocchi in a large saucepan of boiling salted water for 2–3 minutes, or according to the instructions on the packet. Drain well.

5 Stir the garlic and gnocchi into the marrow. Season and then place the greaseproof paper over the marrow and return to the oven for 5 minutes (the weights are not necessary).

6 Just before serving, sprinkle the top with a little chopped fresh basil.

BAKED MARROW IN PARSLEY SAUCE

THIS IS A REALLY GLORIOUS WAY WITH A SIMPLE AND MODEST VEGETABLE. TRY TO FIND A SMALL, FIRM AND UNBLEMISHED MARROW FOR THIS RECIPE, AS THE FLAVOUR WILL BE SWEET, FRESH AND DELICATE. YOUNG MARROWS DO NOT NEED PEELING; MORE MATURE ONES DO.

SERVES FOUR

INGREDIENTS
    1 small young marrow, about 900g/2lb
    30ml/2 tbsp olive oil
    15g/½oz butter
    1 onion, chopped
    15ml/1 tbsp plain flour
    300ml/½ pint/1¼ cups milk
      and single cream mixed
    30ml/2 tbsp chopped fresh parsley
    salt and freshly ground black pepper

1 Preheat the oven to 180°C/350°F/ Gas 4 and cut the marrow into pieces measuring about 5 x 2.5cm/2 x 1in.

2 Heat the oil and butter in a flameproof casserole and fry the onion over a gentle heat until very soft.

3 Add the marrow and sauté for 1–2 minutes and then stir in the flour. Cook for a few minutes, then stir in the milk and cream mixture.

4 Add the parsley and seasoning, stir well and then cover and cook in the oven for 30–35 minutes. If liked, remove the lid for the final 5 minutes of cooking to brown the top. Alternatively, serve the marrow in its rich pale sauce.

COOK'S TIP
Chopped fresh basil or a mixture of basil and chervil also tastes good in this dish.

CUCUMBER AND TROUT MOUSSE

*THIS IS A VERY LIGHT, REFRESHING MOUSSE, MAKING THE MOST OF THE CLEAN TASTE OF CUCUMBER.
SERVE IT AS A STARTER OR FOR A LIGHT LUNCH WITH A GREEN SALAD. YOU COULD ALSO ARRANGE A
CHERVIL LEAF OR A VERY THIN LEMON SLICE ON THE TOPPING.*

SERVES SIX

INGREDIENTS
   1 small cucumber
   2–3 smoked trout fillets, about
     175g/6oz total weight
   115g/4oz fromage frais
   15ml/1 tbsp powdered gelatine
   150ml/¼ pint/⅔ cup vegetable stock
   12–14 pimiento stuffed olives, sliced
   30ml/2 tbsp lemon juice
   5ml/1 tsp finely chopped fresh
     tarragon
   150ml/¼ pint/⅔ cup whipping cream
   2 egg whites
   salt and freshly ground black pepper
   peeled prawns and lettuce leaves,
     to garnish
For the topping
   15ml/1 tbsp powdered gelatine
   90ml/6 tbsp vegetable stock

1 Lightly oil six ramekin dishes. To prepare the topping, take one quarter of the cucumber and slice thinly. Sprinkle the gelatine over the stock, leave to soak for a few minutes and then place over a saucepan of simmering water and stir until completely dissolved.

2 Spoon a little of the gelatine mixture into each dish and arrange two or three cucumber slices on top. Put in the fridge to set. Pour over the remaining gelatine mixture and return to the fridge to set.

3 To make the mousse, peel and very finely dice the remaining cucumber and put in a bowl. Flake the fish, discarding the skin and any bones and add to the cucumber. Beat in the fromage frais.

4 Sprinkle the gelatine over 30ml/2 tbsp of water in a bowl and leave to soak for a few minutes. Place over a saucepan of simmering water and stir until dissolved.

5 Heat the stock. Stir in the dissolved gelatine and leave until cool but not set. Pour over the trout and stir in the olives, lemon juice, tarragon and seasoning.

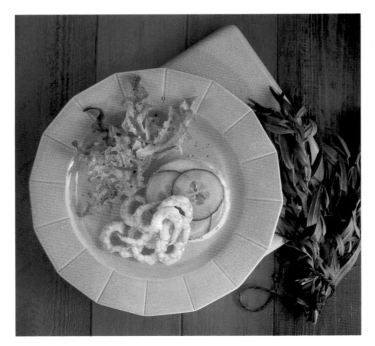

6 Lightly whip the cream and whisk the egg whites until stiff. Fold the cream into the trout mixture, followed by the egg whites. Spoon the mousse into the ramekin dishes, levelling the surface. Cover and chill for 1–2 hours and then unmould on to serving plates.

7 Garnish with a few peeled prawns and serve with lettuce leaves and any remaining tarragon.

LOOFAH AND AUBERGINE RATATOUILLE

LOOFAHS HAVE A SIMILAR FLAVOUR TO COURGETTES AND CONSEQUENTLY TASTE EXCELLENT WITH AUBERGINES AND TOMATOES. BE SURE TO USE VERY YOUNG LOOFAHS AND ALSO ENSURE THAT YOU PEEL AWAY THE ROUGH SKIN, AS IT CAN BE SHARP.

SERVES FOUR

INGREDIENTS

1 large or 2 medium aubergines
450g/1lb young loofahs or
  sponge gourds
1 large red pepper, cut into
  large chunks
225g/8oz cherry tomatoes
225g/8oz shallots, peeled
10ml/2 tsp ground coriander
60ml/4 tbsp olive oil
2 garlic cloves, finely chopped
a few coriander leaves
salt and freshly ground black pepper

1 Cut the aubergine into thick chunks and sprinkle the pieces with salt. Set aside in a colander for about 45 minutes and then rinse well under cold running water and pat dry.

2 Preheat the oven to 220°C/425°F/ Gas 7. Peel and slice the loofahs into 2cm/¾in pieces. Place the aubergine, loofah and pepper pieces, together with the tomatoes and shallots in a roasting pan which is large enough to take all the vegetables in a single layer.

3 Sprinkle with the ground coriander and olive oil and then scatter the chopped garlic and coriander leaves on top. Season to taste.

4 Roast for about 25 minutes, stirring the vegetables occasionally, until the loofah is golden brown and the peppers are beginning to char at the edges.

CHOCOLATE ZUCCHINI CAKE

THE RECIPE FOR THIS MOIST CHOCOLATE CAKE FLAVOURED WITH ZUCCHINI, OR COURGETTES, COMES FROM AMERICA. ALTHOUGH AN UNLIKELY COMBINATION, IT IS A DELICIOUS VARIATION WELL WORTH TRYING.

SERVES FOUR TO SIX

INGREDIENTS
    115g/4oz margarine
    130ml/4½fl oz/½ cup sunflower oil
    115g/4oz caster sugar
    225g/8oz soft brown sugar
    3 eggs, beaten
    130ml/4½fl oz/½ cup milk
    350g/12oz plain flour
    10ml/2 tsp baking powder
    60ml/4 tbsp cocoa powder
    2.5ml/½ tsp ground allspice
    450g/1lb courgettes, peeled
     and grated
    5ml/1 tsp vanilla essence
    225g/8oz plain chocolate dots

1 Preheat the oven to 190°C/375°F/
Gas 5 and line a 23 x 33cm/9 x13in
baking tin with non-stick baking paper.

2 Cream the margarine, oil and sugars
together until light and fluffy, then
gradually beat in the eggs and milk.

3 Sift the flour, baking powder, cocoa
powder and ground allspice together and
fold gently into the mixture.

4 Stir in the grated courgettes and
vanilla essence and spoon the mixture
into the prepared tin. Smooth the top
using a palette knife and sprinkle the
chocolate dots over the top.

5 Bake in the oven for 35–45 minutes
until the cake is firm and a knife comes
out clean. Cut into squares while still
warm and then leave to cool.

PUMPKIN AND HAM FRITTATA

A FRITTATA IS AN ITALIAN VERSION OF THE SPANISH TORTILLA, A SUBSTANTIAL OMELETTE MADE OF EGGS AND VEGETABLES. ALTHOUGH FRITTATAS ARE SOMETIMES EATEN COLD, THIS ONE TASTES BETTER WARM OR HOT, SERVED WITH CRUSTY BREAD.

SERVES FOUR

INGREDIENTS
30ml/2 tbsp sunflower oil
1 large onion, chopped
450g/1lb pumpkin, chopped into
   bite-size pieces
200ml/7fl oz/scant 1 cup chicken
   stock
115g/4oz smoked ham, chopped
6 eggs
10ml/2 tsp chopped fresh marjoram
salt and freshly ground black pepper

1 Preheat the oven to 190°C/375°F/Gas 5 and oil a large shallow ovenproof dish. Heat the oil in a large frying pan and fry the onion for 3–4 minutes until softened.

2 Add the pumpkin and fry over a brisk heat for 3–4 minutes, stirring frequently. Stir in the stock, cover and simmer over a gentle heat for 5–6 minutes until the pumpkin is slightly tender. Add the ham.

3 Pour the mixture into the prepared dish. Beat the eggs with the marjoram and a little seasoning. Pour into the dish and then bake for 20–25 minutes until the frittata is firm and lightly golden.

GAZPACHO

GAZPACHO IS A CLASSIC SPANISH SOUP. IT IS POPULAR ALL OVER SPAIN BUT NOWHERE MORE SO THAN IN ANDALUCIA, WHERE THERE ARE HUNDREDS OF VARIATIONS. IT IS A COLD SOUP OF TOMATOES, TOMATO JUICE, GREEN PEPPER AND GARLIC, WHICH IS SERVED WITH A SELECTION OF GARNISHES.

SERVES FOUR

INGREDIENTS
  1.5kg/3–3½lb ripe tomatoes
  1 green pepper, seeded and roughly chopped
  2 garlic cloves, crushed
  2 slices white bread, crusts removed
  60ml/4 tbsp olive oil
  60ml/4 tbsp tarragon wine vinegar
  150ml/¼ pint/⅔ cup tomato juice
  good pinch of sugar
  salt and freshly ground black pepper
  ice cubes, to serve
For the garnishes
  30ml/2 tbsp sunflower oil
  2–3 slices white bread, diced
  1 small cucumber, peeled and finely diced
  1 small onion, finely chopped
  1 red pepper, seeded and finely diced
  1 green pepper, seeded and finely diced
  2 hard-boiled eggs, chopped

1 Skin the tomatoes, then quarter them and remove the cores.

2 Place the pepper in a food processor and process for a few seconds. Add the tomatoes, garlic, bread, olive oil and vinegar and process again. Add the tomato juice, sugar, seasoning and a little extra tomato juice or cold water and process. The consistency should be thick but not too stodgy.

3 Pour into a bowl and chill for at least 2 hours but no more than 12 hours, otherwise the textures deteriorate.

4 To prepare the bread cubes to use as a garnish, heat the oil in a frying pan and fry them over a moderate heat for 4-5 minutes until golden brown. Drain well on kitchen paper.

5 Place each garnish in a separate small dish, or alternatively arrange them in rows on a large plate.

6 Just before serving, stir a few ice cubes into the soup and then spoon into serving bowls. Serve with the garnishes.

TOMATO AND BASIL TART

IN FRANCE, PÂTISSERIES DISPLAY MOUTH-WATERING SAVOURY TARTS IN THEIR WINDOWS. THIS IS A VERY SIMPLE YET EXTREMELY TASTY TART MADE WITH RICH SHORTCRUST PASTRY, TOPPED WITH SLICES OF MOZZARELLA CHEESE AND TOMATOES AND ENRICHED WITH OLIVE OIL AND BASIL LEAVES.

SERVES FOUR

INGREDIENTS
    150g/5oz mozzarella,
      thinly sliced
    4 large tomatoes, thickly sliced
    about 10 basil leaves
    30ml/2 tbsp olive oil
    2 garlic cloves, thinly sliced
    sea salt and freshly ground
      black pepper
For the pastry
    115g/4oz plain flour
    50g/2oz butter or margarine
    1 egg yolk
    pinch of salt

1 To prepare the pastry, mix together the flour and salt, then rub in the butter and egg yolk. Add enough cold water to make a smooth dough and knead lightly on a floured surface. Place in a plastic bag and chill for about 1 hour.

2 Preheat the oven to 190°C/375°F/ Gas 5. Remove the pastry from the fridge and allow about 10 minutes for it to return to room temperature and then roll out into a 20cm/8in round. Press into the base of a 20cm/8in flan dish or tin. Prick all over with a fork and then bake in the oven for about 10 minutes until firm but not brown. Allow to cool slightly. Reduce the oven temperature to 180°C/350°F/ Gas 4.

3 Arrange the mozzarella slices over the pastry base. On top, arrange a single layer of the sliced tomatoes, overlapping them slightly. Dip the basil leaves in olive oil and arrange them on the tomatoes.

4 Scatter the garlic on top, drizzle with the remaining olive oil and season with a little salt and a good sprinkling of black pepper. Bake for 40–45 minutes, until the tomatoes are well cooked. Serve hot.

ITALIAN ROAST PEPPERS

SIMPLE AND EFFECTIVE, THIS DISH WILL DELIGHT ANYONE WHO LIKES PEPPERS. IT CAN BE EATEN EITHER AS A STARTER SERVED WITH FRENCH BREAD, OR AS A LIGHT LUNCH WITH COUSCOUS OR RICE.

SERVES FOUR

INGREDIENTS
   4 small red peppers, halved, cored
      and seeded
   30–45ml/2–3 tbsp capers, chopped
   10–12 black olives, pitted
      and chopped
   2 garlic cloves, finely chopped
   50–75g/2–3 oz mozzarella, grated
   25–40g/1–1½oz fresh white
      breadcrumbs
   120ml/4fl oz/½ cup white wine
   45ml/3 tbsp olive oil
   5ml/1 tsp finely chopped fresh mint
   5ml/1 tsp chopped fresh parsley
   freshly ground black pepper

1 Preheat the oven to 180°C/350°F/ Gas 4 and butter a shallow ovenproof dish. Place the peppers tightly together in the dish and sprinkle over the chopped capers, black olives, garlic, mozzarella and breadcrumbs.

2 Pour over the wine and olive oil and then sprinkle with the mint, parsley and freshly ground black pepper.

3 Bake for 30–40 minutes until the topping is crisp and golden brown.

SWEET PEPPER CHOUX WITH ANCHOVIES

THE RATATOUILLE VEGETABLES IN THIS DISH ARE ROASTED INSTEAD OF STEWED, AND HAVE A WONDERFUL AROMATIC FLAVOUR. ANY COMBINATION OF RED, GREEN OR YELLOW PEPPERS CAN BE USED. FOR VEGETARIANS, OMIT THE ANCHOVIES.

SERVES SIX

INGREDIENTS
300ml/½ pint/1¼ cups water
115g/4oz butter or margarine
150g/5oz plain flour
4 eggs
115g/4oz Gruyère or Cheddar cheese,
   finely diced
5ml/1 tsp Dijon mustard
salt

For the filling
3 peppers; red, yellow and green
1 large onion, cut into eighths
   or sixteenths
3 tomatoes, peeled and quartered
1 courgette, sliced
6 basil leaves, torn in strips
1 garlic clove, crushed
30ml/2 tbsp olive oil
about 18 black olives, pitted
45ml/3 tbsp red wine
175ml/6fl oz/¾ cup passata or puréed
   canned tomatoes
50g/2oz can anchovy fillets, drained
salt and freshly ground black pepper

1 Preheat the oven to 240°C/475°F/ Gas 9 and grease six individual oven-proof dishes. To prepare the filling, halve the peppers, discard the seeds and core and cut into 2.5cm/1in chunks.

2 Place the peppers, onion, tomatoes and courgette in a roasting tin. Add the basil, garlic and olive oil, stirring so the vegetables are well coated. Sprinkle with salt and pepper and then roast for about 25–30 minutes until the vegetables are just beginning to blacken at the edges.

3 Reduce the oven temperature to 200°C/400°F/Gas 6. To make the choux pastry, put the water and butter together in a large saucepan, heat until the butter melts. Remove from the heat and add all the flour at once. Beat well with a wooden spoon for about 30 seconds until smooth. Allow to cool slightly.

4 Beat in the eggs, one at a time, and then continue beating until the mixture is thick and glossy. Stir in the cheese and mustard, then season with salt and pepper. Spoon the mixture around the sides of the prepared dishes.

5 Spoon the vegetables into a large mixing bowl, together with any juices or scrapings from the base of the pan. Add the olives and stir in the wine and passata or puréed tomatoes. (Or you can stir these into the roasting tin but allow the tin to cool slightly otherwise the liquid will boil and evaporate.)

6 Divide the pepper mixture between the six dishes and arrange the drained anchovy fillets on top. Bake in the oven for about 25–35 minutes until the choux pastry is puffy and golden. Serve hot with a fresh green salad.

EGGS FLAMENCO

A VARIATION OF THE POPULAR BASQUE DISH PIPERADE, THE EGGS ARE COOKED WHOLE INSTEAD OF BEATING THEM BEFORE ADDING TO THE PEPPER MIXTURE. THE RECIPE IS KNOWN AS CHAKCHOUKA IN NORTH AFRICA AND MAKES A GOOD LUNCH OR SUPPER DISH.·

SERVES FOUR

INGREDIENTS
2 red peppers
1 green pepper
30ml/2 tbsp olive oil
1 large onion, finely sliced
2 garlic cloves, crushed
5–6 tomatoes, peeled and chopped
120ml/4fl oz/½ cup puréed canned
    tomatoes or tomato juice
good pinch of dried basil
4 eggs
40ml/8 tsp single cream
pinch of cayenne pepper (optional)
salt and freshly ground black pepper

1 Preheat the oven to 180°C/350°F/Gas 4. Seed and thinly slice the peppers. Heat the olive oil in a large frying pan. Fry the onion and garlic gently for about 5 minutes, stirring, until softened.

2 Add the peppers to the onion and fry for 10 minutes. Stir in the tomatoes and tomato purée or juice, the basil and seasoning. Cook gently for a further 10 minutes until the peppers are soft.

3 Spoon the mixture into four ovenproof dishes, preferably earthenware. Make a hole in the centre and break an egg into each. Spoon 10ml/2 tsp cream over the yolk of each egg and sprinkle with a little black pepper or cayenne, as preferred.

4 Bake in the oven for 12–15 minutes until the white of the egg is lightly set. Serve at once with chunks of crusty warm French or Spanish bread.

SPINACH AND PEPPER PIZZA

MAKES TWO 30cm/12in PIZZAS

INGREDIENTS
450g/1lb fresh spinach
60ml/4 tbsp single cream
25g/1oz Parmesan cheese, grated
15ml/1 tbsp olive oil
1 large onion, chopped
1 garlic clove, crushed
½ green pepper, seeded and thinly
   sliced
½ red pepper, seeded and thinly sliced
175–250ml/6–8fl oz/¾–1 cup passata
   sauce or puréed tomatoes
50g/2oz black olives, pitted and
   chopped
15ml/1 tbsp chopped fresh basil
175g/6oz mozzarella, grated
175g/6oz Cheddar cheese, grated
salt
For the dough
25g/1oz fresh yeast or 15ml/1 tbsp
   dried yeast and 5ml/1 tsp sugar
about 225ml/7fl oz/⅞ cup warm water
350g/12oz strong white flour
30ml/2 tbsp olive oil
5ml/1 tsp salt

1 To make the dough, cream together the fresh yeast and 150ml/¼ pint/⅔ cup of the water and set aside until frothy. If using dried yeast, stir the sugar into 150ml/¼ pint/⅔ cup water, sprinkle over the yeast and leave until frothy.

2 Place the flour and salt in a large bowl, make a well in the centre and pour in the olive oil and yeast mixture. Add the remaining water, mix to make a stiff but pliable dough. Knead on a lightly floured surface for about 10 minutes until smooth and elastic.

3 Shape the dough into a ball and place in a lightly oiled bowl, cover with clear film and leave in a warm place for about 1 hour until it has doubled in size.

4 To prepare the topping, cook the spinach over a moderate heat for 4–5 minutes until the leaves have wilted. Strain and press out the excess liquid. Place in a bowl and mix with the cream, Parmesan cheese and salt to taste.

5 Heat the oil in a frying pan and fry the onion and garlic over a moderate heat for 3–4 minutes until the onion has slightly softened. Add the peppers and continue cooking until the onion is lightly golden, stirring regularly.

6 Preheat the oven to 220°C/425°F/ Gas 7. Knead the dough briefly on a lightly floured surface. Divide the dough and roll out into two 30cm/12in rounds.

7 Spread each base with the passata sauce or puréed tomatoes. Add the onions and peppers and then spread over the spinach mixture. Scatter the olives and basil leaves and sprinkle with the mozzarella and Cheddar cheese.

8 Bake in the oven for 15–20 minutes, or until the crust is lightly browned and the top is beginning to turn golden. Allow to cool slightly before serving.

ENCHILADAS <u>WITH</u> HOT CHILLI SAUCE

IN MEXICO, CHILLIES APPEAR IN ALMOST EVERY SAVOURY DISH, EITHER IN THE FORM OF CHILLI POWDER OR CHOPPED, SLICED OR WHOLE. BY MEXICAN STANDARDS, THIS IS A LOW-HEAT VERSION OF THE POPULAR CHICKEN ENCHILADAS. IF YOU LIKE YOUR FOOD HOT, ADD EXTRA CHILLIES TO THE SAUCE.

SERVES FOUR

INGREDIENTS

- 8 wheat tortillas
- 175g/6oz Cheddar cheese, grated
- 1 onion, finely chopped
- 350g/12oz cooked chicken, cut into small chunks
- 300ml/½ pint/1¼ cups soured cream
- 1 avocado, sliced and tossed in lemon juice, to garnish

For the *salsa picante*

- 1–2 green chillies
- 15ml/1 tbsp vegetable oil
- 1 onion, chopped
- 1 garlic clove, crushed
- 400g/14oz can chopped tomatoes
- 30ml/2 tbsp tomato purée
- salt and freshly ground black pepper

3 Preheat the oven to 180°C/350°F/ Gas 4 and butter a shallow ovenproof dish. Take one tortilla and sprinkle with a good pinch of cheese and chopped onion, about 40g/1½oz of chicken and 15ml/1 tbsp of *salsa picante*. Pour over 15ml/1 tbsp of soured cream, roll up and place, seam side down, in the dish. Make seven more enchiladas.

4 Pour the remaining *salsa* over the top and sprinkle with the remaining cheese and onion. Bake in the oven for about 25–30 minutes until the top is golden. Serve with the remaining soured cream either poured over, or in a separate jug, and garnish with the sliced avocado.

1 To make the *salsa picante*, cut the chillies in half lengthways and carefully remove the cores and seeds. Slice the chillies very finely. Heat the oil in a frying pan and fry the onion and garlic for about 3–4 minutes until softened. Add the tomatoes, tomato purée and chillies. Simmer gently, uncovered, for about 12–15 minutes, stirring frequently.

2 Pour the sauce into a food processor or blender, and process until smooth. Return to the heat and cook very gently, uncovered, for a further 15 minutes. Season to taste then set aside.

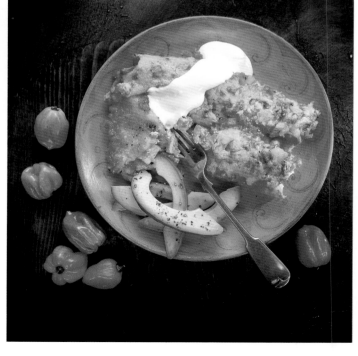

HOT SOUR CHICK-PEAS

THIS DISH, KHATTE CHOLE, IS EATEN AS A SNACK ALL OVER INDIA, SOLD BY ITINERANT STREET VENDORS. THE HEAT OF THE CHILLIES IS TEMPERED PARTLY BY THE CORIANDER AND CUMIN, WHILE THE LEMON JUICE ADDS A WONDERFUL SOURNESS.

SERVES FOUR

INGREDIENTS

350g/12oz chick-peas, soaked
  overnight
60ml/4 tbsp vegetable oil
2 medium onions, very finely chopped
225g/8oz tomatoes, peeled and finely
  chopped
15ml/1 tbsp ground coriander
15ml/1 tbsp ground cumin
5ml/1 tsp ground fenugreek
5ml/1 tsp ground cinnamon
1–2 hot green chillies, seeded
  and finely sliced
about 2.5cm/1in fresh root ginger,
  grated
60ml/4 tbsp lemon juice
15ml/1 tbsp chopped fresh coriander
salt

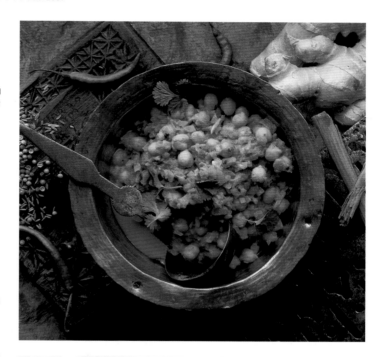

1 Drain the chick-peas and place them in a large saucepan, cover with water and bring to the boil. Cover and simmer for 1–1¼ hours until tender, making sure the chick-peas do not boil dry. Drain, reserving the cooking liquid.

2 Heat the oil in a large flameproof casserole. Reserve about 30ml/2 tbsp of the chopped onions and fry the remainder in the casserole over a moderate heat for 4–5 minutes, stirring frequently, until tinged with brown.

3 Add the tomatoes and continue cooking over a moderately low heat for 5–6 minutes until soft. Stir frequently, mashing the tomatoes to a pulp.

4 Stir in the coriander, cumin, fenugreek and cinnamon. Cook for 30 seconds and then add the chick-peas and 350ml/12fl oz/1½ cups of the reserved cooking liquid. Season with salt, cover and simmer very gently for about 15–20 minutes, stirring occasionally and adding more cooking liquid if the mixture becomes too dry.

5 Meanwhile, mix the reserved onion with the chilli, ginger and lemon juice.

6 Just before serving, stir the onion and chilli mixture and the coriander into the chick-peas, and adjust the seasoning.

GUACAMOLE

THIS IS QUITE A FIERY VERSION OF A POPULAR MEXICAN DISH, ALTHOUGH PROBABLY NOWHERE NEAR AS HOT AS YOU WOULD BE SERVED IN MEXICO, WHERE IT SEEMS HEAT KNOWS NO BOUNDS!

SERVES FOUR

INGREDIENTS

2 ripe avocados, peeled and stoned
2 tomatoes, peeled, seeded and finely
  chopped
6 spring onions, finely chopped
1–2 chillies, seeded and finely
  chopped
30ml/2 tbsp fresh lime or lemon juice
15ml/1 tbsp chopped fresh coriander
salt and freshly ground black pepper
coriander sprigs, to garnish

1 Put the avocado halves into a large bowl and mash them roughly with a large fork.

2 Add the remaining ingredients. Mix well and season according to taste. Serve garnished with fresh coriander.

PLANTAIN APPETIZER

PLANTAINS ARE A TYPE OF COOKING BANANA WITH A LOWER SUGAR CONTENT THAN DESSERT BANANAS. THEY ARE UNSUITABLE FOR EATING RAW BUT CAN BE USED IN A WIDE RANGE OF DISHES. THIS DELICIOUS ASSORTMENT OF SWEET AND SAVOURY PLANTAINS IS A POPULAR DISH IN AFRICA.

SERVES FOUR

INGREDIENTS
2 green plantains
45ml/3 tbsp vegetable oil
1 small onion, very thinly sliced
1 yellow plantain
½ garlic clove, crushed
salt and cayenne pepper
vegetable oil, for frying

1 Peel one of the green plantains and cut into wafer-thin rounds, preferably using a swivel-headed potato peeler.

2 Heat about 15ml/1 tbsp of the oil in a large frying pan and fry the plantain slices for 2–3 minutes until golden, turning occasionally. Transfer to a plate lined with kitchen paper and keep warm.

3 Coarsely grate the other green plantain and mix with the onion.

4 Heat 15ml/1 tbsp of the remaining oil in the pan and fry the plantain and onion mixture for 2–3 minutes until golden, turning occasionally. Transfer to the plate with the plantain slices.

5 Peel the yellow plantain, cut into small chunks. Sprinkle with cayenne pepper. Heat the remaining oil and fry the yellow plantain and garlic for 4–5 minutes until brown. Drain and sprinkle with salt.

RADICCHIO PIZZA

*THIS UNUSUAL PIZZA TOPPING CONSISTS OF CHOPPED RADICCHIO WITH LEEKS, TOMATOES AND
PARMESAN AND MOZZARELLA CHEESES. THE BASE IS A SCONE DOUGH, MAKING THIS A QUICK AND EASY
SUPPER DISH TO PREPARE. SERVE WITH A CRISP GREEN SALAD.*

SERVES TWO

INGREDIENTS

½ x 400g/14oz can chopped tomatoes
2 garlic cloves, crushed
pinch of dried basil
25ml/1½ tbsp olive oil, plus extra
    for dipping
2 leeks, sliced
100g/3½oz radicchio, roughly
    chopped
20g/¾oz Parmesan, grated
115g/4oz mozzarella cheese, sliced
10–12 black olives, pitted
basil leaves, to garnish
salt and freshly ground black pepper
For the dough
225g/8oz self-raising flour
2.5ml/½ tsp salt
50g/2oz butter or margarine
about 120ml/4fl oz/½ cup milk

1 Preheat the oven to 220°C/425°F/
Gas 7 and grease a baking sheet. Mix the
flour and salt in a bowl, rub in the butter
or margarine and gradually stir in the
milk and mix to a soft dough.

2 Roll the dough out on a lightly floured
surface to make a 25–28cm/10–11in
round. Place on the baking sheet.

3 Purée the tomatoes and then pour
into a small saucepan. Stir in one of the
crushed garlic cloves, together with the
dried basil and seasoning, and simmer
over a moderate heat until the mixture is
thick and reduced by about half.

4 Heat the olive oil in a large frying pan
and fry the leeks and remaining garlic for
4–5 minutes until slightly softened. Add
the radicchio and cook, stirring
continuously for a few minutes, and then
cover and simmer gently for about
5–10 minutes. Stir in the Parmesan
cheese and season with salt and pepper.

5 Cover the dough base with the tomato
mixture and then spoon the leek and
radicchio mixture on top. Arrange the
mozzarella slices on top and scatter over
the black olives. Dip a few basil leaves in
olive oil, arrange on top and then bake
the pizza for 15–20 minutes until the
scone base and top are golden brown.

WARM DUCK SALAD WITH ORANGE

THE DISTINCT, SHARP FLAVOUR OF RADICCHIO, CURLY ENDIVE AND FRESH ORANGES COMPLEMENTS THE RICH TASTE OF THE DUCK TO MAKE THIS A SUPERB DISH. IT IS GOOD SERVED WITH STEAMED NEW POTATOES FOR AN ELEGANT MAIN COURSE.

SERVES FOUR

INGREDIENTS

2 boneless duck breasts
salt
2 oranges
curly endive, radicchio and lamb's
    lettuce
30ml/2 tbsp medium dry sherry
10–15ml/2–3 tsp dark soy sauce

1 Rub the skin of the duck breasts with salt and then slash the skin several times with a sharp knife.

2 Heat a heavy cast iron frying pan and fry the duck breasts, skin side down at first, for 20–25 minutes, turning once, until the skin is well browned and the flesh is cooked to your preference. Transfer to a plate to cool slightly and pour off the excess fat from the pan.

3 Peel the oranges. Separate the oranges into segments and use a knife to remove all the pith, catching the juice in a small bowl. Arrange the salad leaves in a shallow serving bowl.

4 Heat the duck juices in the pan and stir in 45ml/3 tbsp of the reserved orange juice. Bring to the boil, add the sherry and then just enough soy sauce to give a piquant, spicy flavour.

5 Cut the duck into thick slices and arrange over the salad. Pour over the warm dressing and serve.

BAKED CHICORY WITH PARMA HAM

ALTHOUGH CHICORY IS SOMETIMES TOO HARSHLY FLAVOURED FOR SOME PEOPLE'S TASTES, SIMMERING IT BEFORE BRAISING ELIMINATES ANY BITTERNESS SO THAT THE FLAVOUR IS PLEASANTLY MILD.

SERVES FOUR

INGREDIENTS
    4 heads of chicory
    25g/1oz butter
    250ml/8fl oz/1 cup vegetable
      or chicken stock
    4 slices Parma ham
    75g/3oz mascarpone cheese
    50g/2oz Emmenthal or Cheddar
      cheese, sliced
    salt and freshly ground black pepper

4 Remove the chicory using a slotted spoon. Lay out the Parma ham slices and place one piece of chicory on each of the slices. Roll up and place, side by side, in a single layer in the prepared dish.

5 Simmer the stock until it is reduced by about half and then remove from the heat. Stir in the mascarpone cheese and pour the sauce over the chicory. Lay the slices of Emmenthal or Cheddar cheese over the top and bake in the oven for about 15 minutes until the top is golden and the sauce is bubbling.

1 Preheat the oven to 180°C/350°F/ Gas 4. Grease an ovenproof dish. Trim the chicory and remove the central core.

2 Melt the butter in a large saucepan and gently sauté the chicory over a moderate heat for 4–5 minutes, turning occasionally, until the outer leaves begin to turn transparent.

3 Add the stock and a little seasoning, bring to the boil and then cover and simmer gently for 5–6 minutes until the chicory is almost tender.

ROCKET AND GRILLED CHÈVRE SALAD

FOR THIS RECIPE, LOOK OUT FOR CYLINDER-SHAPED GOAT'S CHEESE FROM A DELICATESSEN OR FOR SMALL ROLLS THAT CAN BE CUT INTO HALVES, WEIGHING ABOUT 50G/2OZ. SERVE ONE PER PERSON AS A STARTER OR DOUBLE THE RECIPE AND SERVE TWO EACH FOR A LIGHT LUNCH.

SERVES FOUR

INGREDIENTS
    about 15ml/1 tbsp olive oil
    about 15ml/1 tbsp vegetable oil
    4 slices French bread
    45ml/3 tbsp walnut oil
    15ml/1 tbsp lemon juice
    salt and freshly ground black pepper
    225g/8oz cylinder-shaped goat's
        cheese
    generous handful of rocket leaves
    about 115g/4oz curly endive
For the sauce
    45ml/3 tbsp apricot jam
    60ml/4 tbsp white wine
    5ml/2 tsp Dijon mustard

1 Heat the two oils in a frying pan and fry the slices of French bread on one side only, until lightly golden. Transfer to a plate lined with kitchen paper.

4 Preheat the grill a few minutes before serving the salad. Cut the goat's cheese into 50g/2oz rounds and place each piece on a croûton, untoasted side up. Place under the grill and cook for 3–4 minutes until the cheese melts.

5 Toss the rocket and curly endive in the walnut oil dressing and arrange attractively on four individual serving plates. When the cheese croûtons are ready, arrange on each plate and pour over a little of the apricot sauce.

2 To make the sauce, heat the jam in a small saucepan until warm but not boiling. Push through a sieve, into a clean pan, to remove the pieces of fruit, and then stir in the white wine and mustard. Heat gently and keep warm until ready to serve.

3 Blend the walnut oil and lemon juice and season with a little salt and pepper.

CHINESE LEAVES AND MOOLI WITH SCALLOPS

A SPEEDY STIR-FRY MADE USING CHINESE CABBAGE, MOOLI AND SCALLOPS. BOTH THE MOOLI AND CHINESE LEAVES HAVE A PLEASANT CRUNCHY "BITE". YOU NEED TO WORK QUICKLY, SO HAVE EVERYTHING PREPARED BEFORE YOU START COOKING.

SERVES FOUR

INGREDIENTS
    10 prepared scallops
    60–75ml/4–5 tbsp vegetable oil
    3 garlic cloves, finely chopped
    1cm/½in piece fresh root ginger,
      finely sliced
    4–5 spring onions, cut lengthways
      into 2.5cm/1in pieces
    30ml/2 tbsp medium dry sherry
    ½ mooli (daikon radish), cut into
      1cm/½in slices
    1 Chinese cabbage, chopped
      lengthways into thin strips
For the marinade
    5ml/1 tsp cornflour
    1 egg white, lightly beaten
    pinch of white pepper
For the sauce
    5ml/1 tsp cornflour
    45ml/3 tbsp oyster sauce

1 Rinse the scallops and separate the corals from the white meat. Cut each scallop into 2–3 pieces and slice the corals. Place them on two dishes.

2 For the marinade, blend together the cornflour, egg white and white pepper. Pour half over the scallops and the rest over the corals. Leave for 10 minutes.

3 To make the sauce, blend the cornflour with 60ml/4 tbsp water and the oyster sauce and set aside.

4 Heat about 30ml/2 tbsp of the oil in a wok, add half of the garlic and let it sizzle, and then add half the ginger and half of the spring onions. Stir-fry for about 30 seconds and then stir in the scallops (not the corals).

5 Stir-fry for ½–1 minute until the scallops start to become opaque and then reduce the heat and add 15ml/ 1 tbsp of the sherry. Cook briefly and then spoon the scallops and the cooking liquid into a bowl and set aside.

6 Heat another 30ml/2 tbsp of oil in the wok, add the remaining garlic, ginger and spring onions and stir-fry for 1 minute. Add the corals, stir-fry briefly and transfer to a dish.

7 Heat the remaining oil and add the mooli. Stir-fry for about 30 seconds and then stir in the cabbage. Stir-fry for about 30 seconds and then add the oyster sauce mixture and about 60ml/4 tbsp water. Allow the cabbage to simmer briefly and then stir in the scallops and corals, together with all their liquid and cook briefly to heat through.

RADISH, MANGO AND APPLE SALAD

RADISH IS A YEAR-ROUND VEGETABLE AND THIS SALAD CAN BE SERVED AT ANY TIME OF YEAR, WITH ITS CLEAN, CRISP TASTES AND MELLOW FLAVOURS. SERVE WITH SMOKED FISH, SUCH AS ROLLS OF SMOKED SALMON, OR WITH CONTINENTAL HAM OR SALAMI.

SERVES FOUR

INGREDIENTS
   10–15 radishes
   1 dessert apple, peeled cored and
     thinly sliced
   2 celery stalks, thinly sliced
   1 small ripe mango, peeled and cut
     into small chunks
For the dressing
   120ml/4fl oz/½ cup soured cream
   10ml/2 tsp creamed horseradish
   15ml/1 tbsp chopped fresh dill
   salt and freshly ground black pepper
   sprigs of dill, to garnish

3 Cut through the mango lengthways either side of the stone. Make even criss-cross cuts through each side section. Take each one and bend it back to separate the cubes. Remove the mango cubes with a small knife and add to the bowl. Pour the dressing over the vegetables and fruit and stir gently so that all the ingredients are coated in the dressing. When ready to serve, spoon the salad into an attractive salad bowl and garnish with sprigs of dill.

1 To prepare the dressing, blend together the soured cream, horseradish and dill in a small jug or bowl and season with a little salt and pepper.

2 Top and tail the radishes and then slice them thinly. Add to a bowl together with the thinly sliced apple and celery.

STUFFED MUSHROOMS

THIS IS A CLASSIC MUSHROOM DISH, STRONGLY FLAVOURED WITH GARLIC. USE FLAT MUSHROOMS OR FIELD MUSHROOMS THAT ARE SOMETIMES AVAILABLE FROM FARM SHOPS.

<u>SERVES FOUR</u>

INGREDIENTS
   450g/1lb large flat mushrooms
   butter, for greasing
   about 75ml/5 tbsp olive oil
   2 garlic cloves, minced or very
      finely chopped
   45ml/3 tbsp finely chopped fresh
      parsley
   40–50g/1½–2oz fresh white
      breadcrumbs
   salt and freshly ground black pepper
   sprig of flat leaf parsley, to garnsh

1 Preheat the oven to 180°C/350°F/ Gas 4. Cut off the mushroom stalks and reserve on one side.

2 Arrange the mushroom caps in a buttered shallow dish, gill side upwards.

COOK'S TIP
The cooking time for the mushrooms depends on their size and thickness. If they are fairly thin, cook for slightly less time. They should be tender but not too soft when cooked. If a stronger garlic flavour is preferred, do not cook the garlic before adding it to the breadcrumb mixture.

3 Heat 15ml/1 tbsp of oil in a frying pan and fry the garlic briefly. Finely chop the mushroom stalks and mix with the parsley and breadcrumbs. Add the garlic, seasoning and 15ml/1tbsp of the oil. Pile a little of the mixture on each mushroom.

4 Add the remaining oil to the dish and cover the mushrooms with buttered greaseproof paper. Bake for about 15–20 minutes, removing the paper for the last 5 minutes to brown the tops. Garnish with a sprig of flat leaf parsley.

BOEUF EN CROÛTE WITH MUSHROOM FILLING

A DUXELLES FILLING OF FINELY-CHOPPED MUSHROOMS, SHALLOTS, GARLIC AND PARSLEY IS THE CLASSIC FILLING FOR BOEUF EN CROÛTE. THESE INDIVIDUAL VERSIONS ARE GOOD SERVED WITH BOILED OR STEAMED NEW POTATOES AND A GREEN VEGETABLE.

SERVES FOUR

INGREDIENTS
   4 fillet steaks, about
      115–150g/4–5oz each
   a little Dijon mustard
   25g/1oz butter
   275g/10oz puff pastry
   25g/1oz fresh white breadcrumbs
   beaten egg, for glazing
   salt and freshly ground black pepper
   sprigs of parsley or chervil, to garnish
For the duxelles filling
   25g/1oz butter
   4 shallots, finely chopped
   1–2 garlic cloves, crushed
   225–275g/8–10oz flat mushrooms,
      finely chopped
   15ml/1 tbsp finely chopped parsley

1 Preheat the oven to 220°C/425°F/ Gas 7. Rub a little mustard over each of the steaks and season with pepper. Melt the butter in a heavy-based frying pan and fry the steaks for about 1–2 minutes each side, so that they are browned on the outside but still red in the centre. Transfer to a plate to cool.

2 To make the filling, melt the butter and fry the shallots and garlic briefly. Stir in the finely chopped mushrooms.

3 Fry over a fairly high heat for about 3–4 minutes, stirring, until the juices run. Lower the heat and cook gently for 4–5 minutes until the mixture is dry. Add the parsley and seasoning and cool.

4 Cut the pastry into four and roll out each piece very thinly to a 18cm/7in square. Cut the corners from each square and spread a spoonful of the mushroom mixture in the centre. Top with a steak and sprinkle with a spoonful of fresh breadcrumbs.

5 Bring the sides of the pastry up to the centre and seal with water. Place seam side down on a baking sheet. Decorate with pastry trimmings and brush each with beaten egg. Bake for about 20 minutes, until golden brown. Serve garnished with parsley or chervil.

GNOCCHI WITH OYSTER MUSHROOMS

GNOCCHI MAKE AN UNUSUAL AND PLEASANT ALTERNATIVE TO PASTA. THEY ARE BLAND ON THEIR OWN BUT BRING OUT THE FLAVOUR OF THE OYSTER MUSHROOMS IN THIS DISH WHILE THEIR SOFT TEXTURE CONTRASTS WITH THE FIRMNESS OF THE MUSHROOMS.

SERVES FOUR

INGREDIENTS
225g/8oz oyster mushrooms
15ml/1 tbsp olive oil
1 medium onion, finely chopped
1 garlic clove, crushed
4 plum tomatoes, peeled and chopped
45–60ml/3–4 tbsp vegetable stock
  or water
salt and freshly ground black pepper
2 x 300g/11oz packet plain potato
  gnocchi
a good knob of butter
10ml/2 tsp chopped fresh parsley
Parmesan cheese, cut in shavings,
  to serve

1 Trim the mushrooms and tear into smaller pieces, if they are large. Heat the oil in a large frying pan and fry the onion and garlic over a low heat for about 4–5 minutes until softened but not browned.

2 Increase the heat, add the mushrooms to the pan and sauté for about 3–4 minutes, stirring constantly.

3 Stir in the chopped tomatoes, stock or water and seasoning and then cover and simmer for about 8 minutes until the tomatoes are very soft and reduced to a pulp. Stir occasionally.

4 Cook the gnocchi in a large pan of salted boiling water for 2–3 minutes (or according to the instructions on the packet) then drain well and toss with the butter. Place in a large warmed serving bowl and stir in the chopped parsley.

5 Pour the mushroom and tomato mixture over the top, stir briefly and sprinkle with the Parmesan cheese.

COOK'S TIP
If the mushrooms are very large, the stalks are likely to be tough, therefore they should be discarded. Always tear rather than cut oyster mushrooms.

SEAFOOD AND OYSTER MUSHROOM STARTER

THIS DISH IS REMARKABLY QUICK TO PREPARE. IT CAN BE MADE INTO A MORE SUBSTANTIAL DISH BY STIRRING 275-350G/10-12OZ COOKED PASTA SHELLS INTO THE SAUCE AT THE END.

SERVES FOUR

INGREDIENTS
15ml/1 tbsp olive oil
15g/½oz butter
1 garlic clove, crushed
175g/6oz oyster mushrooms,
  halved or quartered
115–175g/4–6oz peeled prawns
115g/4oz cooked mussels, optional
juice of ½ lemon
15ml/1 tbsp medium dry sherry
150ml/¼ pint/⅔ cup double cream
salt and freshly ground black pepper

1 Heat the oil and butter in a frying pan and sauté the garlic for a few minutes, then add the mushrooms. Cook over a moderate heat for 4–5 minutes until soft, stirring from time to time.

2 Reduce the heat and stir in the prawns, mussels and lemon juice. Cook for 1 minute, stirring continuously. Stir in the sherry and cook for 1 minute.

3 Add the cream and cook gently until heated through but not boiling. Taste and adjust the seasoning and then spoon into warmed serving dishes. Serve immediately with chunks of Italian bread.

TAGLIATELLE FUNGI

THE MUSHROOM SAUCE IS QUICK TO MAKE AND THE PASTA COOKS VERY QUICKLY; BOTH NEED TO BE COOKED AS NEAR TO SERVING AS POSSIBLE SO CAREFUL COORDINATION IS REQUIRED. PUT THE PASTA IN TO COOK WHEN THE MASCARPONE CHEESE IS ADDED TO THE SAUCE.

SERVES FOUR

INGREDIENTS
  about 50g/2oz butter
  225–350g/8–12oz chanterelles
    or other wild mushrooms
  15ml/1 tbsp plain flour
  150ml/¼ pint/⅔ cup milk
  90ml/6 tbsp crème fraîche
  15ml/1 tbsp chopped fresh parsley
  275g/10oz fresh tagliatelle
  olive oil
  salt and freshly ground black
    pepper

1 Melt 40g/1½oz of the butter in a frying pan and fry the mushrooms for about 2–3 minutes over a gentle heat until the juices begin to run, then increase the heat and cook until the liquid has almost evaporated. Transfer the mushrooms to a bowl using a slotted spoon.

2 Stir in the flour, adding a little more butter if necessary, and cook for about 1 minute, and then gradually stir in the milk to make a smooth sauce.

3 Add the crème fraîche, parsley, mushrooms and seasoning and stir well. Cook very gently to heat through and then keep warm while cooking the pasta.

4 Cook the pasta in a large saucepan of boiling water for 4–5 minutes (or according to the instructions on the packet). Drain well, toss in a little olive oil and then turn on to a warmed serving plate. Pour the mushroom sauce over and serve immediately.

COOK'S TIP
Chanterelles are a little tricky to wash, as they are so delicate. However, since these are woodland mushrooms, it's important to clean them thoroughly. Hold each one by the stalk and let cold water run under the gills to dislodge hidden dirt. Shake gently to dry.

SHIITAKE FRIED RICE

SHIITAKE MUSHROOMS HAVE A STRONG MEATY MUSHROOMY AROMA AND FLAVOUR. THIS IS A VERY EASY RECIPE TO MAKE, AND ALTHOUGH IT IS A SIDE DISH IT CAN ALMOST BE A MEAL IN ITSELF.

SERVES FOUR

INGREDIENTS

2 eggs
45ml/3 tbsp vegetable oil
350g/12oz shiitake mushrooms
8 spring onions, sliced diagonally
1 garlic clove, crushed
½ green pepper, chopped
25g/1oz butter
175–225g/6–8oz long grain rice, cooked
15ml/1 tbsp medium dry sherry
30ml/2 tbsp dark soy sauce
15ml/1 tbsp chopped fresh coriander
salt

1 Beat the eggs with 15ml/1 tbsp cold water and season with a little salt.

2 Heat 15ml/1 tbsp of the oil in a wok or large frying pan, pour in the eggs and cook to make a large omelette. Lift the sides of the omelette and tilt the wok so that the uncooked egg can run underneath and be cooked. Roll up the omelette and slice thinly.

3 Remove and discard the mushroom stalks if tough and slice the caps thinly, halving them if they are large.

4 Heat 15ml/1 tbsp of the remaining oil in the wok and stir-fry the spring onions and garlic for 3–4 minutes until softened but not brown. Transfer them to a plate using a slotted spoon.

5 Add the pepper, stir-fry for about 2–3 minutes, then add the butter and the remaining 15ml/1 tbsp of oil. As the butter begins to sizzle, add the mushrooms and stir-fry over a moderate heat for 3–4 minutes until soft.

6 Loosen the rice grains as much as possible. Pour the sherry over the mushrooms and then stir in the rice.

7 Heat the rice over a moderate heat, stirring all the time to prevent it sticking. If the rice seems very dry, add a little more oil. Stir in the reserved onions and omelette slices, the soy sauce and coriander. Cook for a few minutes until heated through and serve.

COOK'S TIP

Unlike risotto, for which rice is cooked along with the other ingredients, Chinese fried rice is always made using cooked rice. If you use 175–225g/6–8oz uncooked long grain, you will get about 450–500g/16–20oz cooked rice, enough for four people.